THE *Savvy Girl's* GUIDE

TO THRIVING BEYOND NARCISSISTIC ABUSE

CORISSA STEPP

Copyright © 2025 by Corissa Stepp

The Savvy Girl's Guide to Thriving Beyond Narcissistic Abuse

All rights reserved.

No part of this work may be used or reproduced, transmitted, stored, or used in any form or by any means graphic, electronic, or mechanical, including but not limited to photocopying, recording, scanning, digitizing, taping, Web distribution, information networks or information storage and retrieval systems, or in any manner whatsoever without prior written permission from the publisher.

In this world of digital information and rapidly-changing technology, some citations do not provide exact page numbers or credit the original source. We regret any errors, which are a result of the ease with which we consume information.

The author of this book does not dispense medical advice or prescribe the use of any technique as a form of treatment for physical, emotional, or medical problems without the advice of a physician, either directly or indirectly. The intent of the author is only to offer information of a general nature to help the reader in the quest for well-being. In the event the reader uses any of the information in this book for self or others, which is a constitutional right, the author and the publisher assume no responsibility for the actions of the reader.

No AI Training: Without in any way limiting the author's and publisher's exclusive rights under copyright, any use of this publication to train generative artificial intelligence (AI) or Large Language Model (LLM) technologies to generate text is expressly prohibited.

Edited by: Amy Delcambre and Laurie Knight
Cover Design by: Corissa Stepp

An Imprint for GracePoint Publishing (www.GracePointPublishing.com)

GracePoint Matrix, LLC
624 S. Cascade Ave, Suite 201, Colorado Springs, CO 80903
www.GracePointMatrix.com Email: Admin@GracePointMatrix.com
SAN # 991-6032

A Library of Congress Control Number has been requested and is pending.

ISBN: (Paperback) 978-1-961347-89-2
eISBN: 978-1-966346-41-8

Books may be purchased for educational, business, or sales promotional use.
For distribution queries contact Sales@IPGbook.com
For non-retail bulk order requests contact Orders@GracePointPublishing.com

*For Tyler and Everett, my precious boys,
and every woman who has ever suffered in silence from
the insidious impact of narcissistic abuse*

Table of Contents

Introduction 1

Part One:
NARCISSISM, NARCISSISTIC BEHAVIORS, AND THE NARCISSISTIC ABUSE CYCLE

Chapter One: What IS a Narcissist? And Are They Born That Way?..13
Chapter Two: The Tactics of a Narcissist 32
Chapter Three: The Cycle of Abuse 41

Part Two:
A TALE OF NARCISSISTIC ABUSE

Chapter Four: Idealization—The Beginning 51
Chapter Five: Devaluation and Discard—The Abuse 69
Chapter Six: Hoover—Wait, Come Back! 81
Chapter Seven: Conclusion and Reflection— Empowered Goodbye 93

Part Three:
DEEP DIVE INTO NARCISSISTIC TRAUMA, DYSFUNCTIONAL FAMILY DYNAMICS, AND THE WOUNDS THEY LEAVE BEHIND

Chapter Eight: How Do We End Up in These Toxic Relationships? .97
Chapter Nine: Defining Trauma, Trauma Bonds, and the Four Trauma Responses 107
Chapter Ten: Is It Possible for a Narcissist to Change?............. 117
Chapter Eleven: The Golden Child, the Scapegoat, and the Caregiver All Walk into a Bar 137
Chapter Twelve: The Roles of Attachment Wounds 145
Chapter Thirteen: Symptoms of Narcissistic Abuse 151

Part Four:
HEALING

Chapter Fourteen: Aftermath of a Narcissistic Relationship and Post-separation Abuse 157
Chapter Fifteen: The Key to Healing 167
Chapter Sixteen: Picking Up the Pieces: Rediscovering Who You Are 174
Chapter Seventeen: Reparenting the Inner Child 185
Chapter Eighteen: How to Stop Attracting Narcissists 195
Chapter Nineteen: Boundaries, Boundaries, Boundaries 200
Conclusion 210
About the Author 219

Introduction

This book is dedicated to a topic that I am very passionate about because it is something that I, myself, have overcome and am still healing from. This book is different from most, as in part two, I will share a story to demonstrate how easy it is to find yourself in a toxic relationship, and I will illustrate the cycle of abuse. It doesn't matter how smart you are or how savvy or experienced you are in relationships. It doesn't even matter if you had what felt like a normal childhood or a traumatic one. We can all fall into these traps very easily. I want to break the shame that surrounds victims of abusive relationships.

Sadly, most people do not even realize the relationship they are in is toxic until the relationship is either over or limping along on life support. My hope is that illuminating the cycle of abuse through storytelling in part two will make you more aware of the patterns of behavior. In part three, you will learn how and why you may have ended up in this type of a relationship and then ultimately, in part four, you'll learn how to heal and move forward.

Narcissistic abuse can include six different types of abuse, but it may vary from relationship to relationship. Not all six may be part of the abuse you experience in a narcissistic relationship. However, it is important to be aware of the different types so you can better understand what you are experiencing.

The six different types of abuse are emotional, psychological, physical, verbal, sexual, and financial. For purposes of clarity, I will share some of the behaviors of each of these different types of abuse for better understanding. It is important to note that it can be hard to delineate between emotional, psychological, and verbal abuse; therefore, I've done my best to break each of them down.

Emotional Abuse
- Constant criticism
- Shaming
- Minimizing or diminishing
- Trivialization
- Invalidation
- Catastrophizing
- Scapegoating
- Coercive control
- Extreme jealousy
- Blame and guilt
- Exploitation or blackmailing
- Neglect

Psychological Abuse
- Gaslighting
- Isolation
- Triangulation
- Intimidation
- Manipulation
- Humiliation
- Silent treatment
- Withholding affection, attention, money
- Stalking
- Dismissing

Verbal Abuse
- Name-calling
- Yelling, shouting, or raging
- Threats
- Cursing at you
- Excessive sarcasm
- Mocking
- Belittling

Sexual Abuse
- Restricting or not allowing use of birth control without consent

- Unwanted kissing or touching
- Rough or violent sexual acts without consent
- Threatening, pressuring, or coercing someone to participate in an unwanted sexual act or touching inappropriately
- Marital rape or sex without consent or while incapacitated (while intoxicated or sleeping)

Financial Abuse
- Restricting or threatening to restrict partner's access to money
- Stealing possessions or money
- Misuse of joint funds/children's bank accounts
- False representation by using partner's (or children's) identity to fraudulently open credit cards, bank accounts, lines of credit, second mortgages, etc. in their name or jointly
- Misuse of power of attorney to claim mental instability or incapacitation of otherwise healthy spouse to control assets
- Taking unnecessary financial risk without disclosure
- Controlling all the finances or being intentionally obscure about where the assets are held or how they are being spent to keep partner in the dark to control all the money/investments
- Unexplained withdrawals of money from accounts
- Hiding assets or money
- Control of all financial decisions, without consent
- Berating, belittling, attacking partner for expenditures or expenses

I will not be addressing physical abuse; however, please note that if you are enduring physical abuse in your relationship, it is of the utmost important that you have an exit strategy in place so that you can safely disentangle yourself from your abuser without risking further harm or putting your life at stake. Please reach out to your local domestic violence center for support to ensure you have everything you need for a safe escape and a fresh start.

I also would be remiss if I did not provide a trigger warning given the sensitivity of the subject matter we are discussing in this book. At times, the content may illicit a strong emotional response. If that is the case, I would encourage you to put it down and focus on your breathing until you feel calm or to go for a walk outside before picking up where you left off. If you feel safe and comfortable, allow yourself to fully experience whatever emotions are bubbling up and journal to allow them to be processed and released.

Before we continue, perhaps you might also like to know a little bit about me, the author. Please allow me to properly introduce myself!

My name is Corissa Stepp and I am a Certified Somatic Trauma Informed Coach™ and Narcissistic Abuse Specialist™ whose passion lies in empowering fiercely independent and intuitive women in releasing their emotional triggers and trauma so they may nurture peaceful, loving relationships.

In my most important role, I am a mom to two wonderful boys, Tyler and Everett, who at the time of this writing are fourteen and twelve years old, respectively.

When I'm not working, doing laundry, or trying to keep up with my kids' ceaseless appetites and sports schedules, you'll find me hiking on a nearby trail, singing at the top of my lungs, or planning my next adventure.

While I have trained and studied narcissistic abuse and trauma for the purpose of coaching other women through the recovery process, I have also experienced it firsthand and, sadly, in way too many significant relationships than I care to admit throughout my life. As a result, it is a topic area that I have researched passionately and studied closely.

Like many women who have attracted these types of toxic personalities into their lives, I spent the majority of my life playing small, biting my tongue, and stuffing down my emotions in order to be liked, loved, and accepted by others.

As such, I am a recovering people pleaser, codependent, and survivor of narcissistic abuse. I was conditioned to believe other people's emotions were more important than my own, nothing I was ever going through was as important as what someone else was going through, love was hard and had to be earned, and that achieving or striving for the next shiny, gold object was the way in which I would receive recognition, validation, approval, and affection.

If I had to trace the beginning of my people pleasing and perfectionist tendencies back to my earliest memory, I would say it would be from when I was around eight years old.

We were at my cousin's high school graduation party if my memory serves me correctly, and my sister and I were fighting. My dad turned around from the front seat of the car because he had likely had enough and yelled, "Corissa, you're older; you should know better."

I remember sitting there feeling deeply hurt and dumbfounded. I remember replying with I am sure quite a bit of sass and incredulity, "But I'm only fifteen months older than her. We're practically the same age!" He just reiterated that I should still know better.

From that point forward, I think I began to see that because I was older, it was my job to be more responsible than my sister, more mature, and most certainly know how to behave, which was to be nothing less than perfect. It also wasn't okay to be a child; I had to act more like an adult, even if I was only eight or nine years old.

While this story may seem a bit overdramatic, I believe these little memories become cornerstones for the beliefs we hold about ourselves and that we tuck away in our memory's filing cabinet so we can later recall and heal the wounds they may have inflicted.

Later, in high school, I recall sleeping over at a friend's house and having to leave in the morning to go to my aunt and uncle's house because it was Easter. My friend was Greek and celebrated Greek Easter, so I wasn't infringing on their family holiday by sleeping over, and let's face it, I was way past the age of having my parents hide the Easter eggs.

Before my mother arrived to pick me up, I put on the dress she had bought and expected me to wear for the occasion. When I stepped out of the bathroom, my friends started laughing. Not just giggling but the rolling-on-the-floor, couldn't-catch-their-breath kind of laughing.

They teased me, saying I looked like a businesswoman because the dress was way too mature for a fifteen-year-old girl.

I've always had a pretty good sense of humor and had a flair for the dramatic (after all, I was in musical theater), so I decided to play up the insult by really stepping into the role. I decided I would wear my hair in a bun at the nape of my neck to complete the look of a high-powered businesswoman.

My mother was not entirely amused when she picked me up, even though I tried to convincingly explain that my frizzy hair would fare better in a bun due to the rainy weather.

Silently, however, I was cursing her under my breath because while yes, I had aspirations of being a high-powered businesswoman, I did not want to start dressing like one at fifteen years old!!

Ever the people pleaser, I didn't fight the battle or express my unhappiness or embarrassment. I kept it to myself. After all, since I was eight, I enjoyed the praise and admiration I received for being more mature for my age, so why not dress and act like it?

While these two incidents seem harmless, looking back on them, I can see how the theme of pleasing others had been pervasive throughout my life, beginning in childhood. I can also see how I felt I *had* to be someone I was not (someone who was more mature) and how I felt I was responsible for way more than was age appropriate. I learned to manage other people's emotions at the expense of my own.

As I matured, I continued to slowly hand over my power to anyone whom I loved and trusted, assuming they had my best interests at heart.

Never in a million years did I think that I wanted something different from what they wanted for me. Their dreams were my dreams, their expectations were my expectations, their happiness was my happiness, their sadness, anger, anxiousness, worry, etc. were all mine as well.

What I didn't realize was that I wasn't living my life *for* me, *as me*. Our society normalizes codependency through the music we listen to, the movies we watch, and the stories we read, so I thought nothing of it.

I've now spent the last several years trying to undo these patterns and break the cycles. It's been quite the journey, and I've learned a lot about behavioral patterns, childhood trauma, narcissistic personalities, and myself.

Recovering from people pleasing and realizing I am not responsible for anyone else's emotions or meeting their needs has been uncomfortable at times.

At the same time, it has been empowering to know that I am only responsible for *my* feelings and meeting my own needs first before I try to meet the needs of others.

Learning how to set boundaries and enforce them has been another challenge, along with getting to know who I am, not who others imagine, expect, or want me to be.

While I will not discuss in detail my longest narcissistic relationship out of respect for the other person and to protect others who may be impacted, just please know that I have been where you have been. I have experienced what you have experienced, and I have spent a lot of time researching, understanding, and learning as much as I can so I can now help others on the same path. This book is a testament to that.

I will say that I understand now why this most significant narcissist and I were attracted to each other, where we made mistakes, and why it was an experience I needed to have.

At this point in the journey, I am able to genuinely say I will always be grateful to him because he has been one of my *greatest* teachers. Through the experience of the relationship, I not only learned all about the insidious tactics, behaviors, and traits, and the impact of narcissistic abuse, but I also discovered who I am, what my purpose is, and how I can use the power of the past and the wisdom of the present to liberate my future. It is what propelled me into training and certifying as a Somatic Trauma Informed Coach™ and Narcissistic Abuse Specialist™.

For that, I will be forever grateful. The work I do feels incredibly meaningful and fulfilling in a way my career in the hedge fund industry never did.

As you read on, please remember that narcissists are human beings, too. They are not monsters, nor are they terrible people. They usually have a lot of good in them as well. If they were despicable 100 percent of the time, none of us would have loved them in the first place nor would we have stayed in the relationship for as long as we did. You'll understand more as I redefine what narcissism is in chapter one.

It is important to share that while I do not regret the relationship and have forgiven my narcissistic ex, I will continue to hold him accountable for his behavior and also take accountability for my contribution to the relationship dynamics.

While I am able to forgive and offer compassion for the ex-narcissist(s) in my life, please know it has taken a lot of hard work, healing, and recovery to get here. So, please do not feel guilty or upset if you are not ready to do the same.

It is always best to allow yourself to feel *all* your emotions, and if anger toward the narcissist is what you are feeling right now, then allow it, feel it, and express it in a safe space. Women have been conditioned to believe that anger is not a safe emotion. However, anger can be a catalytic emotion that propels you *out* of the toxic relationship, so it may be absolutely necessary for you to feel in order to move forward.

I know how utterly exhausting it is to wear a mask and pretend everything is okay while enduring emotional and psychological abuse. When I decided that the mask had become way too heavy to continue to hold, and I was ready to set it down, I felt like I had crumbled beneath its weight. It left me with a lost sense of who I was. Picking up the pieces has been both exhausting and deeply challenging, but through the healing process, I have been able to build resilience.

So, if you feel drained, chronically frustrated, and unhappy, know it is reason enough to end the relationship if you are able to cut ties. If you need to maintain some semblance of a relationship, then be sure to set clear and strong boundaries so you can minimize any further abuse.

Regardless, the intention of this book isn't to help you discern if you should stay in or leave your relationship, but rather to help you heal, recover, and courageously move forward in whatever way you see fit that feels aligned for you, in the right timing.

Since I am not comfortable sharing my personal story of narcissistic abuse, I have instead written the story in part two, which is based on a culmination of factual events in my life and the lives of clients, friends, etc., as well as my knowledge and understanding of narcissistic behaviors, patterns, and traits. The names and circumstances have been changed to protect the identities of those involved, and the purpose is to illustrate how subtle narcissistic abuse is and how it begins, oftentimes, below your level of awareness.

Many of you may understand the definition of an overt narcissist as depicted by Jon Hamm's character in *Mad Men*. It is someone who is overly charismatic, grandiose, charming, and has a high degree of self-confidence. A person who believes their needs are the most important and getting them met supersedes any vows or promises they make, and this is often at the expense of others.

Please know that throughout this book I am not attempting to diagnose a narcissist, but rather use the blanket term "narcissist" to describe the unhealthy personality traits and behaviors an individual may have adapted as a result of their own deep wounding, which likely occurred during childhood or young adulthood.

However, just as there are many shades of gray, there are many variations of how narcissistic personalities present themselves. One of the hardest to discern is that of the covert narcissist, which is why I chose to make the lead narcissist a covert narcissist in part two.

First, let's go into a bit more detail about what a narcissist is, the tactics they use, and what the cycle of abuse looks like.

Part One

NARCISSISM, NARCISSISTIC BEHAVIORS, AND THE NARCISSISTIC ABUSE CYCLE

Chapter One

WHAT IS A NARCISSIST? AND ARE THEY BORN THAT WAY?

For the purposes of this book, I will be using the term *narcissist* as a blanket term to describe someone who has adapted toxic or unhealthy patterns of behavior to overcome some sort of emotional or psychological pain that has deeply wounded them. This wound was inflicted, most likely, during childhood or early adulthood. There are ten different types of narcissists, each representative of different expressions of narcissistic behavior, traits, and patterns; however, first, let's discuss how someone may be clinically diagnosed with narcissistic personality disorder, or NPD.

According to the *DSM-5*, otherwise known as the *Diagnostic and Statistical Manual of Mental Disorders, Fifth Edition*, there are only nine traits that are used to diagnose someone with NPD.

These nine traits are as follows:
1. Has a grandiose sense of self-importance (e.g., exaggerates achievements and talents, expects to be recognized as superior without commensurate achievements)
2. Is preoccupied with fantasies of unlimited success, power, brilliance, beauty, or ideal love
3. Believes that they are "special" and unique and can only be understood by, or should associate with, other special or high-status people (or institutions)
4. Requires excessive admiration

5. Has a sense of entitlement (i.e., unreasonable expectations of especially favorable treatment or automatic compliance with their expectations)
6. Is interpersonally exploitative (i.e., takes advantage of others to achieve their own ends)
7. Lacks empathy: is unwilling to recognize or identify with the feelings and needs of others
8. Is often envious of others or believes that others are envious of him or her
9. Shows arrogant, haughty behaviors or attitudes.[1]

According to the *DSM-5*, in order to be diagnosed with NPD, a person would need to present with at least five of the criteria above. However, in understanding narcissistic behaviors and traits, there are more than nine characteristics that narcissists present. As a matter of fact, there are many characteristics and traits, and we will discuss them in further detail in Chapter Eight: How Do We End Up in These Toxic Relationships?

For now, we are going to focus on the ten different types of narcissists so you may have a better understanding of the many ways in which they present.

Let's first lay down some basic defining traits of all narcissists regardless of their type:
- They are created, not born (more on that below).
- They are deeply insecure.
- They have deep inner wounds from childhood.
- They believe in a finite amount of power—you either have it or you don't.
- They use manipulative tactics.
- They are toxic and abusive.
- They lack self-awareness.
- They have little to no empathy.
- They lack remorse and will not take accountability for their actions.
- They struggle to regulate their emotions.
- They feel safest controlling others.

---

[1] "Narcissistic Personality Disorder," PsychDB, updated January 27, 2024, https://www.psychdb.com/personality/narcissistic.

- They are emotionally immature.

With this basis of understanding, we can now discuss the four main types of narcissists and the three different subtypes.

Four Main Types

The main types may be the ones you are most familiar with along with the first subtype since they are the terms you may hear more often in discussions around narcissists.

Grandiose or Classic

Grandiose narcissists, often referred to as "classic" narcissists, are the most recognizable form of narcissistic personality disorder as they encapsulate all nine traits listed in the DSM-5. They are defined by an exaggerated sense of self-importance, an unrelenting need for admiration, and a profound lack of empathy. Grandiose narcissists are bold, overt, and unapologetic in their behavior.

Their confidence and charisma often make a striking first impression, drawing others in with their charm. However, beneath their seemingly self-assured exterior lies a fragile ego. They are deeply sensitive to criticism or rejection, and even minor feedback can trigger defensiveness, anger, or retaliatory behavior. This combination of outward superiority and inner fragility makes them both magnetic and emotionally exhausting for those around them.

To those who don't know them well, grandiose narcissists often seem larger than life. They present themselves as highly accomplished, talented, or successful and thrive in situations where they can showcase their abilities or achievements. Whether it's commanding a room with their stories or dominating a conversation, they seek to maintain a sense of superiority and control in social interactions.

Their charm and confidence are often mistaken for genuine self-assurance, which can make it difficult to recognize their more harmful traits initially. Many people are captivated by their boldness, mistaking their arrogance for ambition, strength, or importance. Over time, however, the cracks begin to show as their lack of empathy and exploitative tendencies come to the surface.

In romantic relationships, grandiose narcissists are often intoxicating at first. They may overwhelm their partner with attention, gifts, or affection, creating an intense and seemingly ideal connection. This initial phase of overwhelming attention and affection is designed to create dependency and secure the narcissist's constant supply of admiration.

As the relationship progresses, their focus shifts to themselves. They begin to neglect their partner's emotional needs, dismiss their feelings, or criticize their actions. A grandiose narcissist might say things like, "Why can't you be more ambitious?" or, "You used to care about your appearance more." These comments, framed as helpful, honest, or a joke, chip away at their partner's confidence while reinforcing the narcissist's sense of superiority.

They also struggle with boundaries. Infidelity or other betrayals are not uncommon, and when confronted, they are quick to deflect blame onto their partner. Statements like, "If you paid more attention to me, I wouldn't have looked elsewhere," or, "You pushed me away," are typical ways they avoid accountability, leaving their partner feeling both betrayed and responsible for the problems in the relationship.

Grandiose narcissists often gravitate toward leadership roles or high-visibility positions where they can command attention and gain recognition. Initially, they may appear confident, ambitious, and capable, which can help them climb the corporate or social ladder quickly. However, their entitlement and lack of empathy often create tension over time.

They have a tendency to take credit for successes while deflecting blame for failures. For instance, they might say, "If it weren't for me, the project would've fallen apart," while blaming team members for any setbacks. Their dismissiveness toward feedback and unwillingness to collaborate often alienate colleagues, creating a toxic work environment.

Despite their apparent competence, their behavior limits their ability to build trust or foster genuine teamwork. Their focus remains on elevating themselves, often at the expense of those around them, which can lead to long-term dysfunction within teams or organizations.

Grandiose narcissists manipulate others by leveraging their charm, confidence, and ability to twist situations in their favor. In relationships, they often establish control through cycles of idealization and devaluation. Initially, they make their partner feel deeply valued, only to later undermine their confidence through criticism or neglect.

Socially, they dominate interactions, ensuring the focus remains on them. They may dismiss others' contributions or steer conversations back to their own achievements. In professional settings, they often use their charisma to gain favor with superiors while undermining colleagues or taking credit for others' work.

Their lack of empathy and refusal to accept responsibility amplify the harm they cause, as they deflect blame or twist narratives to maintain control and protect their ego. Over time, this manipulation leaves others feeling confused, invalidated, and emotionally drained.

The harm caused by grandiose narcissists lies in their exploitative, one-sided relationships and their ability to undermine the self-worth of those around them. Their charisma and confidence can make them appealing at first, but their entitlement, lack of empathy, and manipulative behaviors often leave lasting emotional damage.

Their constant need for validation and control can erode their partner's self-esteem. The cycle of idealization, criticism, and blame leaves their partner questioning their worth and struggling to regain confidence. Socially, their dismissiveness and arrogance alienate others, creating tension and resentment.

Perhaps the most damaging aspect of grandiose narcissists is their ability to twist reality, making others feel at fault for the harm they cause. This gaslighting not only creates confusion but also makes it difficult for their targets to trust their own perceptions and experiences.

Communal

A communal narcissist is someone who will volunteer their time, energy, resources, or money to help others as a way to seek validation, approval, recognition, and attention from others. It is important to note that their underlying motivation is what truly defines them.

While many people volunteer their time to serve their communities with selfless intentions, communal narcissists operate differently. Their actions are carefully designed to ensure they receive something in return—whether that's praise, admiration, or enhanced status. It's not the act of helping itself that matters to them but the opportunity to receive praise, attention, or recognition for their efforts which boosts their fragile egos and reinforces their sense of importance, superiority, and power.

A communal narcissist will volunteer and take on roles or projects that allow them to appear altruistic, using these opportunities to garner admiration and control the narrative about their character. For example, a communal narcissist may make a large donation to a charitable cause or foundation, not out of generosity, but with the hopes of being honored and celebrated publicly. If they are seen as do-gooders, then they can't possibly be toxic or abusive. They must be trustworthy and noble, or so they want you to believe. It is how this type of narcissist receives validation that they are a good person, despite the fact that they may be manipulative and harmful. It's even better if there are a lot of photo opportunities for the communal narcissist to put their charitable giving or work on display for the world to see.

If their efforts go unnoticed or unappreciated, they may become resentful or passive-aggressive. For a communal narcissist, validation is not optional—it is the fuel that sustains their carefully crafted persona. Their "selflessness" becomes a tool to manipulate others, often by evoking guilt or positioning themselves as indispensable.

This contrasts sharply with someone with altruistic intentions. Genuine acts of service come from compassion and a desire to make a difference, without any expectation of acknowledgment or receiving something in return. Unlike communal narcissists, truly altruistic individuals are not motivated by external validation, but rather an internal sense of fulfillment.

The most notable examples I can provide of communal narcissists would be a priest who is seen as a selfless servant of the community, earning trust and reverence. Yet, he uses this trust and his leadership position (power imbalance) to manipulate and sexually abuse young altar boys to get sexual and power needs met. Or the teacher who is outwardly celebrated as a dedicated educator because she goes above and beyond for her students. Yet, she covertly abuses her power to control and intimidate them when no one is watching. This performative persona helps her feel superior and remain in control, while garnering praise and admiration from colleagues or parents. Or, the nonprofit treasurer who cultivates a reputation for being generous or self-sacrificing. Secretly, they exploit their position by lining their pockets each month from the charity box, believing no one will notice. They justify their actions by feeling entitled to the funds as a reward for their "sacrifices." This could even be the carpooling mom who volunteers to drive her kids and all their neighborhood friends to the community pool every weekend but then gets frustrated and annoyed when no one praises her excessively, despite having been told "thank you" many times over, or complains and gossips to anyone who will listen about how she does so much for others who don't deserve it and how no one does anything for her in return.

The harm caused by communal narcissists lies in their ability to manipulate others while maintaining an outward image of generosity. Their behavior can leave victims feeling guilty, indebted, or questioning their perceptions. For example, a communal narcissist might say, "After all I've done for you, this is how you treat me?" or, "If it weren't for me, where would you even be?" These comments reinforce dependency and diminish the confidence of those around them.

In social or professional settings, communal narcissists often sow division through subtle manipulations, such as comparing their own contributions to others' or by guilt-tripping peers into compliance. Their constant need for acknowledgment can create tension, as others feel overshadowed or undervalued. Over time, their behavior undermines trust and fosters resentment.

Communal narcissists use their perceived altruism to mask their self-serving motives. Their actions, though seemingly generous, are designed to feed their ego and gain admiration, often at the expense of others' well-being.

Vulnerable

A vulnerable narcissist often appears to be sensitive, fragile, or even introverted, giving the impression that they do not like being the center of attention. They may appear more approachable, empathetic, or self-effacing—making them very hard to identify—than the more obvious grandiose narcissist. They, too, however, will have little to no empathy.

You may also hear vulnerable narcissists called "victim" narcissists since they tend to be stuck in patterns of victimhood. They frequently frame themselves as misunderstood, underappreciated, or unfairly treated, using these narratives to elicit sympathy or admiration. Covert narcissists, by definition, are always vulnerable narcissists as they share the same core traits of insecurity, hyper-sensitivity, and subtle manipulation.

Vulnerable narcissists use tactics that are below our level of awareness, making them very difficult to spot. Unlike the overt tactics of grandiose narcissists, their methods of manipulation are much more subtle and insidious, often taking years to detect. They may employ emotional withdrawal, guilt-tripping, or passive-aggressive behaviors to control those around them. This form of manipulation feels more like death by a thousand paper cuts—small, seemingly insignificant actions that, over time, leave behind a gaping emotional wound.

When confronted or criticized, their insecurity manifests as defensiveness, passive-aggressive behavior or even bouts of narcissistic rage. These reactions are often disproportionate to the situation, rooted in their fragile ego and hypersensitivity to perceived slights or rejection.

While they may be subtle and introverted in their ways, vulnerable narcissists often cultivate an image of being the unassuming good guy who everyone likes. Their need to be liked is tied to their fragile sense of self. To bond and connect with others, they may share tales of woe, struggle, or hardship, seeking sympathy and praise for their perceived resilience. Alternatively, they subtly elicit praise or recognition for their good-guy efforts to ensure they cement their carefully constructed persona while serving their deeper need for approval.

This good-guy persona can be particularly disarming, as it contrasts sharply with the harmful behaviors they employ behind closed doors. By maintaining a facade, they can manipulate others while deflecting suspicion and ensuring their reputation remains intact.

Vulnerable narcissists may struggle to hold down a job, often blaming someone else as to why they were let go, fired, or unable to find another job. They may portray themselves as victims of unfair treatment or difficult circumstances, never taking responsibility for their failures.

On the other hand, they may be very successful and appear rather humble and modest. However, they are often quick to claim they are on the verge of getting fired or blame someone or something else for why they are not receiving a promotion, raise, or the recognition they secretly believe they deserve. This mix of humility and victimhood makes their underlying entitlement harder to detect.

One of the most effective tools in a vulnerable narcissist's arsenal is their ability to pull on the levers of fear and guilt to control you. They rarely tell you explicitly what to do or what not to do. Instead, they make statements that sound like concern for your well-being, but subtly fan the flames of your deepest fears and insecurities to get you to comply, give in, or do what they want.

For example, they might say, "I just worry about what might happen to you if we get divorced, you've never been great with money," or "I'll support you either way, are you sure this is the right decision?" These statements create doubt, making you second-guess your decisions, and they can undermine your confidence while nudging you toward the outcome they desire. Over time, this manipulation erodes your autonomy and sense of capability, often without you realizing it.

Don't let the subtlety of their tactics fool you. Being in a relationship with a vulnerable narcissist can be profoundly harmful. Their manipulation often goes undetected for years, leaving you emotionally drained, insecure, and questioning your reality. The invisible wounds they leave behind are not the result of obvious acts of abuse but of countless small, insidious actions that accumulate over time.

What makes them especially dangerous is the contrast between their outward appearance and their internal motivations. To the outside world, they may seem like sensitive, caring individuals, which can leave you feeling isolated and unsupported when you try to explain the harm caused. While others only see the polished, masked version of their persona, you are left to endure the damaging reality of who they truly are.

Malignant

This is the most toxic type of narcissist, who is highly manipulative without any sense of remorse. As a matter of fact, they will often take pleasure in exploiting or hurting others using deliberate, premeditated tactics to achieve their goals. Their cruelty is not incidental; it is calculated and intentional, making their actions all the more chilling.

The malignant narcissist may also show signs of sociopathy and psychopathy, which means they are the most dangerous type as well. This combination of narcissistic grandiosity, lack of empathy, and antisocial tendencies makes them the most destructive and harmful of all the narcissist types.

I have only been in a relationship once with someone who I believe was a malignant narcissist. In my experience, the malignant narcissist is, by far, the most calculated, deceitful, and cunning of the four main types. They know PRECISELY what they are doing, and this awareness makes their actions feel deeply disorienting and painfully intentional.

So much so, that I believe they employ grooming tactics—methods commonly associated with the behaviors of sexual predators, child molesters, and cult leaders. Grooming involves creating a false sense of security and trust to manipulate their target into dependence and vulnerability. Malignant narcissists use this tactic to an extreme degree, cultivating a deep sense of secrecy around the relationship while fostering emotional and psychological dependency. This dependency makes their target far more susceptible to manipulation and abuse. They work to establish an intense emotional intimacy very quickly, luring their target into a false sense of closeness. This tactic creates a profound bond that leaves their victim feeling trapped, isolated, and completely vulnerable to the malignant narcissist's control.

Unlike other types of narcissists, who may rely on narcissistic mirroring to create superficial familiarity or connection, the malignant narcissist takes this much deeper.

Malignant narcissists are uniquely dangerous because they blend their need for dominance with a sadistic streak. They may go beyond simply exploiting others to actively deriving pleasure from their suffering, whether emotional, psychological, or physical. Their manipulative arsenal includes gaslighting, blame shifting, triangulation, and calculated emotional sabotage—all designed to keep their target confused and dependent while elevating their own sense of power and control.

It is important to note that malignant narcissists often exhibit paranoid tendencies, viewing others as threats or obstacles to their superiority. This paranoia can make them exceptionally retaliatory, escalating conflicts to devastating levels if they perceive their ego or authority is challenged.

Malignant narcissists are, without question, the most alarming and chilling type of narcissist. Their ability to charm, manipulate, and dominate with precision and cruelty leaves a trail of devastation for those unlucky enough to cross their path. Understanding their methods is critical to protecting yourself from their harm and finding the strength to break free from their grip.

The Subtypes

Expression Style Subtype

Expression Style Subtype is the most widely known as it defines whether the narcissist is a covert or overt narcissist. It describes how the narcissist behaves to get their needs met.

An overt narcissist will use more obvious and potentially egregious methods that are out in the open for all to see to get their needs met.

A covert narcissist will be much more subtle and shrouded in the ways in which they manipulate others to get their needs met, and this may be done either consciously or subconsciously.

Grandiose and communal narcissists tend to be overt, and vulnerable narcissists are always covert. Malignant narcissists can be either covert or overt. A covert, malignant, sadistic narcissist is perhaps the most dangerous and potentially life-threatening of all.

Value Priorities Subtype

Value Priorities Subtype points to what the narcissist most highly values either in themself or others.

A somatic narcissist is someone who is highly vain and places a significant importance on their appearance, age, and physicality. They often dedicate considerable time to maintaining their looks, whether that's through rigorous workouts at the gym, skincare routines, cosmetic procedures, or admiring themselves in the mirror. To them, their physical appearance is a primary source of their identity and self-worth. For a somatic narcissist, having a trophy wife, husband, or partner is often a priority, as it reinforces their image of success and desirability. They tend to surround themselves with attractive people but may feel threatened by anyone who outshines them, unless associating with someone more attractive serves to elevate their social status or feeds their ego in some way. Beyond their focus on appearance, somatic narcissists may flaunt their lifestyle, highlighting their fitness achievements, designer clothing, or luxury purchases. Their goal is to ensure others perceive them as enviable and superior, often prioritizing outward appearances over deeper, meaningful connections. This fixation on aesthetics can lead to shallow relationships where others are valued for how they contribute to the narcissist's image rather than for who they truly are.

A cerebral narcissist places immense value on intellect and education, often presenting themselves as a know-it-all, and striving to impress others with their intellectual prowess, accomplishments, or position of power. They are deeply driven by a need to be seen as the smartest person in the room. Their sense of superiority stems from their perceived mental abilities, which they view as the defining characteristic that sets them apart from—and above—others. Even if they lack formal education, they may take pride in their success, influence, or ability to outsmart those they perceive as more credentialed or accomplished, like Ivy League graduates. This fuels their belief that they are uniquely gifted, regardless of external qualifications. Cerebral narcissists are drawn to relationships and associations that can help them bolster their status, either socially or professionally. They are drawn to people who can help them climb the corporate ladder or elevate their intellectual image. Relationships are often transactional, as they seek validation or opportunities to assert intellectual dominance rather than fostering mutual connection. In conversation, they tend to monopolize discussions, dismiss differing viewpoints, or use complex language to appear more knowledgeable. Disagreements are often met with condescension or defensiveness, as they view opposing opinions as personal attacks. While their intellect may be impressive, their preoccupation with superiority often leaves others feeling dismissed or undervalued. This dynamic creates relationships where their ego takes precedence over genuine emotional connection, leaving those around them feeling emotionally drained.

Any of the main types of narcissists can be somatic or cerebral.

Extremes of Narcissism Subtype

Extremes of Narcissism Subtype are a special type of narcissist with particularly rare or intense traits. It includes sadistic and inverted narcissists. Sadistic narcissists are a subset of malignant narcissist who derive extreme pleasure in hurting, shaming, and demeaning others. They relish in other people's pain, often finding satisfaction in causing emotional or physical harm. In some cases, their behavior may extend to weird, unusual, or harmful sexual fetishes. Their lack of empathy and enjoyment of others' suffering makes them comparable to sociopaths and psychopaths. Their actions often escalate over time, as their need for control and domination deepens, further isolating and harming their targets.

Inverted narcissists, on the other hand, are a specific type of vulnerable, covert narcissist characterized by low self-confidence and a tendency to remain stuck in victimhood. They may appear quiet and withdrawn, but beneath the surface they are often seething with anger and resentment. Unlike most narcissists, who prioritize getting their needs met, inverted narcissists may engage in self-sacrificial behavior, which can be confusing to those who expect narcissists to be inherently self-serving. However, their self-sacrifice is driven by a deep need for external validation. They are extremely sensitive to criticism, a trait that stems from childhood trauma and a profound abandonment wound. This sensitivity, combined with their need to feel special, often leads them to couple with other narcissists who mirror their self-worth back to them, though this is not always the case. It is essential to distinguish inverted narcissists from people pleasers, as the latter may engage in self-sacrificial behavior out of genuine care or fear of conflict, without the manipulative or validation-seeking motives that characterize narcissism. Inverted narcissists often use self-sacrifice as a tool for control, subtly expecting recognition, admiration, or loyalty in return. Their behaviors are fueled by hidden motives, such as maintaining power over relationships or avoiding feelings of inadequacy. This dynamic can create toxic codependency, as they derive their sense of value from pleasing or accommodating another person, often to their own detriment.

For those who identify as people pleasers, it's important to reflect on your underlying motivations. Genuine people pleasers are typically driven by compassion, fear of conflict, or a desire to maintain harmony, not by an underlying sense of entitlement or a deep need for validation.

As you can see, there are many different types of narcissists. They come in all shapes and sizes. Someone who is a narcissist may also have another personality disorder as well.

Are Narcissists Born or Created?

Narcissists are not born—they are created by their predisposition to genetic traits and the environment in which they grew up.

A narcissist endured what is called narcissistic injury in childhood through dysfunctional family dynamics (which we will cover more in depth in chapter eleven), where they experienced a fracture in their sense of self.

This injury occurs when the narcissist grows up with a negligent, narcissistic, substance-addicted, abusive, or emotionally unsafe caregiver.

If their caregiver was narcissistic, they may have had to adore without judgment or criticism in order to receive approval, validation, or something they ascribe to love. Or the narcissistic parent may have had very black-and-white thinking, called *splitting*, that may be impressed upon the child as values and truths, i.e., people are either good or bad, lovable or unlovable, accepted or rejected, powerful or weak, successful or a failure.

The narcissist may equally have had a parent who overly praised and recognized them for all of their achievements, accomplishments, good looks, or intelligence without providing consistent or unconditional love. In a home where a child is only given attention or "love" because of their achievements, performance, aptitude, or behavior, then the child learns that love is conditional and that the only way they are accepted or loved is when they are being someone their parents approve of, rather than being accepted and loved for who they truly are. This child will grow up to chase love, happiness, and success outside of themselves and adapt traits that help them achieve those things, even if they are disingenuous.

Now, what I have just described may also be true for a co-dependent child. It's important to note that while this experience I have depicted may contribute to a child developing narcissistic tendencies, it might also lead them to become codependent. They may rely upon one or both parents and, later, a partner for approval and validation to support their sense of self-worth, lovability, and value.

When this leads the child toward more narcissistic tendencies, they may learn to boast about their achievements as a way to earn recognition, attention, and love. They may come to believe they are special or entitled because of their accomplishments, building a superficial life focused on maintaining a persona that looks impressive but lacks depth and fulfillment.

Believing their achievements set them apart, they often see themselves as superior to others, which hinders their ability to form meaningful relationships. Lacking self-love and acceptance, they are unable to extend genuine love or acceptance to others. As a result, their relationships are often shallow, with a focus on preserving appearance, even at the expense of those closest to them.

In partnerships, a narcissist may seek out a partner that they perceive as inferior to maintain power and control, or they may initially gravitate toward someone they see as an equal who they believe is deserving of their love and attention. However, if the narcissist begins to feel threatened by their partner's success or intelligence, they may resort to tearing them down to reassert their dominance and protect their fragile ego.

If their caregiver was substance dependent, the emotional environment in the home was likely unpredictable, inconsistent, or devoid of emotional safety. This instability may leave the child with repressed anger and a deep fear of rejection, making them prone to rage and emotional dysregulation as they grow older.

In cases where the child was also expected to adore the addicted caregiver without question and keep the family member's addiction a secret, they may internalize the belief that one can behave however they wish and still deserve love and respect. Over time, this can contribute to entitlement issues, as the child learns to equate love and respect with status or power rather than earned connection.

As adults, they may adopt these distorted beliefs in their own relationships, becoming the parent who demands respect, love, and adoration simply because of their position. For example, they may assert authority with statements like, "You owe me respect because I'm your parent," or "You should listen to me because I'm in charge," while failing to recognize the need for mutual respect and accountability.

If a child grows up with a parent who constantly criticizes, devalues, or belittles them, then the child will potentially learn to pacify the parent by behaving in a way deemed worthy by the parent. The parent accepts the child's behavior only when they behave in the same vein as the parent, and if that parent is a narcissist, well, then the child will exhibit many narcissistic tendencies as well, as a way to stay safe.

Similarly, the child may feel compelled to strive for perfection, believing they must meet impossibly high standards to gain their parent's approval. This drive for perfection is often based on how they perceive themselves through the eyes of their caregiver, creating an unattainable standard they will struggle to achieve.

As they grow older, this need for validation may influence their choice of partner. They might seek someone who makes them look good, who elevates their status, or who helps them achieve the image of the "perfect" life they feel they must attain in order to gain approval. If they lack self-esteem to believe they can achieve success or "perfection" on their own, they may use their partner as a way to fill this void.

This dynamic can lead to manipulative or exploitative behaviors, as the fear of parental rejection or the voice of their own loud inner critic feels too overwhelming to face. To avoid failure and ensure success, they may rationalize using others as a means to an end, prioritizing achievement over authenticity. Over time, this pattern reinforces their dependency on external validation, leaving them disconnected from their own sense of worth.

All of this being said, children of narcissistic parents may grow up to become either narcissists themselves or very empathetic codependents. We will discuss codependency and its relevance to narcissism in Chapter Eight: How Do We End Up in These Toxic Relationships?

A child may also grow up with a caregiver or caregivers who exhibit a blend of all of these traits as well. It is also important to keep in mind that you cannot diagnose a child as a narcissist. They must be much older, closer to adulthood in order to make that determination.

Young children live very much in a "me-centric" world until around the age of eight or nine, when they begin the ten-to-fifteen-year process of differentiating from their family.

During the first seven or eight years, children, according to Richard Barrett of the Barrett Values Centre, are in a state of conforming in terms of their psychological development, and as such, they will likely adapt the behaviors and traits of their parents as a way to feel safe, protected, and accepted.

It is possible that if a child grows up with two narcissistic parents, they may have begun to mirror their parents' narcissistic tendencies as a way to self-preserve by the time they are seven or eight years old. If a child grows up with a narcissistic parent and a codependent parent, then the child may end up conforming their behaviors and traits toward either parent. This is also why narcissism exists on a spectrum. We all have narcissistic tendencies which are necessary for survival; however, the intensity of the traits will determine if a person is harmfully narcissistic or not.

Again, if after reading this, you fear that your child is turning into a narcissist, remember that you cannot make that determination until the child has fully differentiated themselves and their prefrontal cortex has fully developed around the age of twenty-five. There are ways, of course, to prevent your child from developing unhealthy narcissistic traits and behaviors by teaching and modeling empathy and helping them take accountability for their actions. You'll also want to help guide them toward how to correct the behavior, to apologize, and to make amends.

Below is a chart reprinted from Barrett Academy for the Advancement of Human Values, "The Stages of Psychological Development."[2]

Stages of psychological development	Age ranges	Developmental tasks
Serving	60+ years	Contributing to the well-being of future generations, humanity and the planet.
Integrating	50 - 59 years	Connecting with others in unconditional loving relationships to make a difference.
Self-actualising	40 - 49 years	Expressing your true nature by embracing your soul's values and purpose.
Individuating	25 - 39 years	Discovering your true identity by letting go of your fears and your dependence on others.
Differentiating	8 - 24 years	Feeling recognised and respected by establishing yourself in a community that values who you are.

---

2 "The Stages of Psychological Development," Barrett Academy for the Advancement of Human Values, accessed January 30, 2025, https://www.barrettacademy.com/stages-of-psychological-development

Conforming	3 - 7 years	Feeling safe and protected by staying close to kin and your family.
Surviving	Conception to 2 years	Staying alive and physically healthy by getting your survival needs met.

Chapter Two
THE TACTICS OF A NARCISSIST

For narcissists, love is a transaction, and anger can be the weapon when the transaction goes cold. How the anger gets expressed may vary from person to person. There is an arsenal of tools anger employs in order to maintain the control and power in the relationship.

One of these tools is manipulation, but it can also be tactics of verbal, psychological, or emotional abuse.

When narcissists begin to feel insecure in their relationships or about themselves in general, they will resort to whatever tactics they can to regain a sense of control and self-worth. It's important to remember narcissists are deeply wounded and insecure individuals at their core.

Their insecurity often drives a belief that power and worth are finite, leading them to exhibit rigid, all-or-nothing thinking. This perspective can make them view relationships and interactions as zero-sum games, where someone's gain is automatically their loss. As a result, their behaviors are often reactive, self-protective, and manipulative, designed to restore a fragile sense of superiority.

To feel secure and maintain a sense of self-worth, narcissists need to feel in control and superior to others. They achieve this through overt tactics such as belittling, criticizing, diminishing, and devaluing others. However, they can also employ more subtle and covert methods, including manipulation, triangulation, isolation, and accusations, to undermine and control those around them.

Once you become aware of the red flags and tactics of a narcissist, it becomes much easier to recognize when these behaviors are occurring. This newfound awareness makes it difficult to unsee the patterns and nearly impossible to ignore the signs once you've identified them.

Grooming

In the very beginning of a relationship, before the narcissist goes out on a limb and risks rejection, they will often groom their potential partners to lay the foundation for easier manipulation. This is often done by trying to establish familiarity, whether that is through shared experiences or common acquaintances, as well as early testing of boundaries to see how much they are able to get away with. Part of the grooming process often involves testing how naive or trusting the unassuming prospect may be. It may also involve sharing deceptive or false information to pave the way toward further manipulation and to create a false sense of security. In the early stages of the relationship, there is often a willingness to suspend disbelief or give a new suitor the benefit of the doubt. As a result, the individual may readily accept what the narcissist says as truth without questioning it.

Grooming is not often discussed as a tactic in the context of narcissistic abuse, as it is more commonly associated with sexual or child predators. However, narcissists, particularly those who are more conscious and calculated in their behavior, such as malignant narcissists, can and do use grooming to manipulate and control their targets.

This type of premeditated grooming is less characteristic of vulnerable, covert narcissists, who are likely to rely on more subtle forms of manipulation techniques, such as understated love bombing. In contrast, grandiose, overt narcissists tend to employ more extravagant and over-the-top love-bombing techniques, making their grooming tactics far more visible and overwhelming.

Love Bombing

Love bombing is a tactic commonly used in the idealization phase and often serves as its starting point. Love bombing involves excessive flattery and attention, generosity, gushing, and grand gestures. This manipulative tactic is often the easiest to spot, unless it is being employed by a covert narcissist because then it will be much more subtle and harder to detect.

Often, an overt narcissist will come on a little too hot and heavy, too soon. With a covert narcissist, however, you may not recognize this stage. They may only appear consistently attentive or charming. Likely, they will not make grand gestures or buy extravagant gifts to impress you; instead, they will appear more humble, self-deprecating, and subtle.

Every once in a while, the covert narcissist may make a gushing comment or buy you cheap flowers from the supermarket. If you had experienced a lot of toxic relationships before you met this covert narcissist, then that one gushing comment or minimal gift is enough to get you hooked. It may feel like they are filling the holes in your soul, and as a result, it sets you up for accepting breadcrumbs for the entirety of the relationship. Accepting breadcrumbs may have already been a familiar pattern from childhood or past relationships.

Triangulation

Triangulation is a manipulation tactic used to create competition, jealousy, or tension between you and another person, giving the narcissist greater control over you. By driving a wedge between you and someone close, such as a family member, friend, or colleague, they aim to destabilize the relationship. This tactic can lead you to self-isolate or question the other person's intentions, allowing the narcissist to influence your actions, thoughts, and behaviors more easily.

Jealousy can be used in two distinct ways by the narcissist. They may try to make you jealous of someone else, leaving you feeling as though you need to work harder in the relationship to earn their love, validation, or approval. You may feel compelled to become more like this other person in order to keep the narcissist's favor. By inciting your jealousy, the narcissist manipulates you into seeking their approval, which feeds their sense of power and control.

Alternatively, the narcissist might claim to be jealous of someone else to elicit constant reassurance of your love and affection. This can subtly influence your decisions, such as choosing not to go out with friends to avoid making them feel insecure or jealous. You may begin to believe that prioritizing the narcissist over others proves your love for them. Meanwhile, they are simply using jealousy as a way to manipulate and control your actions and behavior.

Both forms of jealousy are insidious tactics designed to stoke the narcissist's ego, making them feel more important and reinforcing their need for power and control.

A narcissist may also inspire competition between you and someone else for their love, approval, and recognition. This dynamic frequently arises in family settings, where a narcissistic parent will manipulate their children into competing for attention, affection, or favor.

In a marriage or partnership, this type of triangulation might manifest when the narcissist accuses you of giving too much attention, affection, or time to the children and not enough to them. They may explain how unimportant they feel since the children were born and that you are too doting, causing you to feel guilty and forcing you into the impossible position of having to choose between your narcissistic partner and your children. In this scenario, a triangle forms between you, your narcissistic partner, and the children.

On the other hand, the narcissist may try to pit you against your children by saying disparaging things about them to make you feel as though it's you two as the parents against the unruly children. In other cases, the narcissist may create the opposite dynamic, aligning themselves with the children and turning them against you, or attempting to alienate you from them altogether.

This last example is what is referred to as parental alienation, which sadly can happen inside of a marriage or post-separation. It is a form of abuse, and it is extremely unhealthy for the children who are unknowingly being used as pawns but also extremely hurtful for the non-narcissistic parent. If you are experiencing this, please seek out the appropriate professional support of a therapist for you and your children, as navigating this dynamic can be overwhelming.

The narcissist may also create tension between you and another person who they deem may have influence over you or who they feel may be on to them and their behaviors. By creating drama and tension, they effectively attempt to place a wedge between you and the other person as a way to isolate you from them. Narcissists thrive on controlling the narrative. If someone else helps you see that your experience might be unhealthy, the narcissist will feel threatened. They want to keep you from questioning the relationship or seeing the truth of their behavior. To protect their control, they'll often try to create distance between you and that person, whether by undermining your connection, limiting your interactions, or planting doubt about their intentions. Triangulation is often used to place a wedge between you and the people closest to you, which leads us to our next manipulation tactic.

Isolation

Triangulation can lead to isolation, so the two can go hand in hand. As we continue to dive into the manipulative tactics of a narcissist, you will begin to become aware of how many of them tend to overlap, adding further confusion to what you may be experiencing.

Isolation tactics involve the narcissist trying to do precisely what it says—isolate you away from your close relationships. Without supportive relationships, the narcissist can control more of the narrative and have more influence on how you think, act, and behave.

It also helps the narcissist avoid being found out for who they are, because if you begin sharing what is happening in your relationship, others may begin to voice concern over how toxic the relationship is and may even expose the narcissist as unsafe.

When you are isolated from the rest of your network, the narcissist can maintain more control and become the center of your world, which is precisely what the narcissist wants. Maybe not all narcissists, but some. This is also how they can control the narrative you start to believe about yourself. If you do not have anyone else highlighting your positive attributes (such as accolades from colleagues at work, recognition for accomplishments, etc.), you can feel even more deeply demoralized, worthless, and unimportant (all of these narratives serve the narcissist). The more disconnected you become from your sense of self and your innate power, the easier it is for them to control you and keep your full attention focused on their needs.

This isolation may also include sabotaging your career pursuits or creating barriers that prevent you from earning a sustainable income, thereby increasing your dependence on them. Relying solely on the narcissist for financial support places you in a position of vulnerability while allowing them to maintain power and control. This dynamic is a form of financial abuse. It's important to remember you have a right to earn an income if you choose to do so.

With all of these tactics, there are many ways in which they can be expressed. For example, the narcissist may pressure you or manipulate circumstances to force you to move away from your family and friends—even during a family crisis—as a way to further isolate and control you.

This is another example of how the isolation tactic can play out, where the narcissist avoids providing any type of emotional support during a difficult time, leaving you isolated and alone in an experience that you may be struggling with.

Silent Treatment

The silent treatment and isolation can also go hand in hand. After a tense conversation or conflict, you may need some time alone, and that is completely normal. The silent treatment, however, especially when it lasts for hours, days, or months on end with absolutely no communication, is emotional abuse.

The narcissist may freeze you out by not even acknowledging your presence. When this happens, it may be their attempt to get you to apologize and take accountability for what happened while not accepting any responsibility on their end.

They likely already know you have a deep fear of abandonment, and by stoking that fear, they can influence how you behave. This might lead you to work even harder to please them, compromise your values, agree to things that make you uncomfortable, or apologize unnecessarily—all in the hope of being accepted or even praised.

This behavior might compel you to beg them not to leave or push you to go to great lengths to meet their needs and keep them happy, often at the expense of your own needs, wants, and desires.

DARVO

DARVO stands for deny, attack, and reverse victim and offender. A narcissist will use this psychologically abusive tactic to avoid taking accountability for their actions. When confronted, they will vehemently deny wrongdoing; shift the focus by attacking you, your character, and your actions (at present or in the past); and project what they did *onto* you. They will make you feel like the offender while positioning themselves as the victim. This tactic may be subtle or highly overt.

If you find yourself often walking away from confrontations or feeling responsible for what happened, then it is possible you are a victim of DARVO. In any type of confrontation, there are two parties responsible. Being able to set boundaries by holding someone else accountable for their actions, while taking responsibility for your own, is healthy. Accepting blame due to guilt and shame or out of fear of abandonment or rejection is not healthy.

Gaslighting: Blame Shifting and Word Mincing

These tactics are used to manipulate and may be used alongside any of the previous ones mentioned.

For informative purposes, gaslighting is the act of convincing you that a sequence of events did not occur the way they did or that you are remembering things incorrectly. Narcissists do this by stirring up doubt and confusion in your mind about what actually happened. You may have been convinced you knew exactly what happened or what was said at the onset, but when you confront the narcissist, you walk away feeling fuzzy about what actually transpired. You may begin to believe that perhaps you *did* recall things incorrectly because they so convincingly muddled the truth and convinced you their version of events was what happened. This is a form of psychological abuse.

The narcissist is distorting the truth (lying or word mincing) to serve their own purpose, which is, of course, to control you and to get you to question your own sense of reality, judgment, intuition, and memory recall. Gaslighting may also include scapegoating, where they blame shift everything onto you, and coercion, where they convince you to do something you don't want to do out of guilt or shame or fear as a result of the thing they blamed you for.

Years of experiencing gaslighting can really disconnect you from your ability to trust yourself, which is precisely what the narcissist desires. The less you trust yourself, the more you will trust *them* and ignore the red flags your intuition is sending to you.

Blame shifting is similar to DARVO in that the narcissist deflects responsibility by projecting the blame onto you or an external circumstance. It's all about denying accountability for their actions. Rather than acknowledging their wrongdoing, they shift focus by blaming you or someone else for causing the situation. Through gaslighting, they manipulate you into believing that you are at fault.

Word mincing occurs when the narcissist twists your words or their own words around to suit their objective, whatever that might be. It may feel as though you are with someone who is bipolar or has multiple personalities. They may say one thing and then turn around and say something completely different and convince you the latter is what they said initially, leaving you confused and possibly frustrated. Over time, you may begin to think you are going crazy or experiencing early onset dementia when, in fact, they are essentially gaslighting you by mincing words.

Narcissistic tactics are designed to confuse, control, and erode your sense of self. Over time, these behaviors can leave you questioning everything, including your own worth, perceptions, and decisions. You may feel trapped in a cycle of self-doubt and emotional exhaustion, as the narcissist's manipulations blur the lines between truth and deception. However, awareness is a powerful tool. By recognizing these tactics for what they are, you can begin to see through the manipulation and reclaim your sense of self. Awareness allows you to identify red flags, set boundaries, and disrupt the narcissist's control, empowering you to protect your emotional well-being and rebuild your confidence. With clarity, you can take back the narrative and regain control of your life.

Chapter Three

The Cycle of Abuse

The cycle of narcissistic abuse consists of four distinct phases. We will identify each phase, and then I'll share a story that illustrates how the cycle unfolds. Recognizing these stages is crucial because it helps you understand what to expect. Knowledge is power—once you're aware of what's happening, you can begin taking steps to disrupt the cycle and reclaim control.

Idealization

The idealization phase, which some may call the love-bombing phase, occurs when the narcissist goes out of their way to charm and court you. They may shower you with attention, affection, gifts, and flattery, making you feel as though you've met your perfect match. Early in the relationship, they may also begin testing your boundaries to see what behaviors you will tolerate, excuse, and accept. To gain control and elicit your empathy, the narcissist may position themselves as the victim, sharing stories that evoke your sympathy.

For grandiose narcissists, this phase often includes grooming tactics to determine whether you'll be an easy target. They employ narcissistic mirroring to appear ideal or even too good to be true, claiming to share your interests or to have had similar life experiences, such as a difficult childhood or challenging relationships. This creates a false sense of familiarity and safety, subtly planting the seeds that will later make it easier for you to excuse and rationalize their bad behavior.

Vulnerable covert narcissists, on the other hand, may present themselves as shy, misunderstood, or wounded souls during this phase. They might share stories of personal struggles or hardships, framing themselves as victims in need of your care and understanding. By appealing to your empathy, they create a dynamic where you feel responsible for their emotional well-being, making it harder to recognize manipulation when it occurs later.

Malignant narcissists may employ a more calculated approach, blending love bombing with subtle tests of control. They might position themselves as protectors or saviors, offering support while carefully laying the groundwork for domination. Their charm can feel intoxicating, but their underlying motivations are deeply predatory.

Despite their differences, the goal of the idealization phase is the same: to draw you in, gain your trust, and create a connection that fosters dependency. Whether through overt charm, victimhood, or calculated manipulation, the narcissist works tirelessly to convince you that they are everything you've been looking for—your soulmate, confidant, or savior.

In long-term relationships, the idealization phase will look slightly different. They may still plan extravagant date nights or overnight trips. They may still send flowers or buy you surprise gifts; however, it's also possible that the flattery, attention, and gifts die down over time. Instead, the narcissist will engage in what I call "manipulative memory recall," where they reminisce about all the great times you two have shared. They may pull out old photo albums or videos on their phone and ask if you remember the events in order to remind you of how great things could be again. The intention behind manipulative memory recall is to inspire hope within you that things will get better or go back to "normal" to keep you in the relationship.

They may also use tactics like "future faking" or baiting, where they paint a vivid picture about all the spectacular things you'll do together in the future, such as the amazing trips you'll take, the dream house you'll buy, or other grand plans designed to win your trust and deepen your emotional investment. The reality is those promises will never come to fruition. Future faking is the narcissist's way of fueling your hope for a more idealistic future, keeping you emotionally invested and stuck in the relationship.

Advice: When you are first getting to know someone, pay attention to how you feel in your body. While it can be very easy to get swept up by all the flattery, attention, and charm, be mindful of how you feel internally. The chemistry between you might feel so intense that it overshadows any red flags. However, if you pay close attention, there will likely be moments when you sense that their words or actions lack genuine emotion or are driven by a hidden agenda. Something will feel *off*. If you feel butterflies in your stomach, it is likely your nervous system alerting you to some perceived danger, not that you have met your Prince Charming. Instead of ignoring the butterflies or thinking they are a sign of true love, *run*. If your new partner seems too good to be true, most likely they are. Also pay attention to how much effort they are putting into actually getting to know you. Are you the one asking all the questions to get to know them and are they only parroting them back to you? Or are they genuinely interested and curious about getting to know you better? Remember, it's not just their words that matter but also their actions.

Devaluation

The devaluation phase involves the narcissist criticizing, demeaning, or belittling you. This may happen covertly with backhanded compliments or outright jabs. It is during this phase that the narcissist will resort to various manipulative tactics, including gaslighting, black-and-white thinking (also known as splitting), triangulation, and word mincing. Their intention in using these tactics, whether consciously or not, is to get you to begin to question and doubt yourself, while also whittling away your self-worth to remain superior and in control.

As previously mentioned, gaslighting is a tactic where the narcissist will rewrite history to reflect a different version of what actually happened, causing you to question whether or not you remembered the incident, conversation, or experience correctly. This may be done very subtly at first and then more overtly later on, when or if the abuse intensifies. It might leave you questioning your sanity

Advice: Write everything down! If you feel like you are stepping out of arguments or conflict feeling confused, doubtful, or unsure of what just happened, then write it down. Write down what you think you remember and what they said happened. Write down everything you can remember and go back to reflect on it to prove to yourself that you are not crazy. You may even wish to keep a daily journal, and keep it somewhere safe, so you have a record and can prove to your doubting mind that you are, in fact, not crazy or suffering from temporary amnesia. I cannot stress enough how important it is that you keep this journal in a safe, secure place. If you need to buy one with a lock on it, do it. If you feel safer journaling in a password-protected app on your phone, then do it. Your safety should be your utmost priority. The last thing you want to happen is to have the narcissist find your journal and read it. It could lead to dire consequences, so please, no matter how savvy you think you are, keep any written record out of their reach.

Discard

Typically, after the devaluation phase, something happens that causes a transition in the relationship. It could be that you set a boundary, or you call the narcissist out on their behavior. Whatever it is, it is essentially viewed by the narcissist as a threat to their power and control, and as such, the relationship will enter either the discard phase or the hoover phase, depending on external factors. For example, has the narcissist found new supply? Or do they believe staying in the relationship will help preserve their self-image or benefit them socially or financially?

The discard phase may not always mean the ending of the relationship. It can take the form of the silent treatment, where the narcissist sulks or is angry for an extended period of time, to remind you that *you* did something wrong. This tactic is meant to provoke your fear of abandonment, giving them the upper hand as you become worried or upset about the possibility of them leaving.

The discomfort or lack of safety created by this unsettling dynamic can lead you to apologize or take accountability for things you didn't even do, simply to restore the harmony. You might find yourself wondering how to make it up to them, trying even harder to please or appease them in hopes of ending the silence.

I urge caution during this phase. Do not self-abandon and sacrifice your truth, needs, wants, values, or authenticity to fix the relationship or keep the peace. Maintaining your sense of self is vital, even in the face of their manipulative tactics.

This may also be the phase where the narcissist abruptly ends the relationship because they've found a new source of narcissistic supply. Alternatively, they may betray or cheat on their partner, keeping one foot in the relationship and the other out the door, hedging their bets.

Advice: You do not deserve to be treated in this way. The silent treatment, when it lasts for an unreasonable amount of time, is a form of emotional abuse. Taking time to yourself after an argument to process your emotions, reflect on what triggered you, and consider how you want to respond is perfectly healthy. Typically, after a few hours or maybe after a good night's sleep, most people feel calmer and ready to reengage in a constructive conversation to resolve the conflict as a couple. This is normal.

With a narcissist, however, the silent treatment may last an entire day or longer. When it extends beyond a reasonable amount of time, or when they refuse to acknowledge your presence or withhold affection, it crosses the line into emotional abuse. This behavior is not about resolving the conflict but about maintaining power and control.

If the silent treatment ends abruptly without any effort from the narcissist to discuss or actively engage in a meaningful dialogue to resolve the presenting issues, it is simply a tactic to exert power and control.

When you attempt to address issues, you may experience even more emotional and verbal abuse. This is their way of manipulating you into shutting down and shutting up, effectively discouraging you from raising current or future issues going forward. This tactic keeps the narcissist in control and you in compliance and silence. Over time, this can feel really isolating and confusing, gradually eroding your ability to use your voice to advocate for yourself.

Conflict is never just one person's fault. Healthy relationships take two people working together to resolve conflict, with both partners sharing accountability. Resolving conflict should feel like a team effort where you're both aligned toward the same goal. It should not involve one person being made to feel guilty, forced to accept all the blame, or pressured to apologize first simply because your partner refuses to accept accountability for their role in the conflict or its resolution.

Hoover

The hoover phase will come after the discard phase, where the narcissist will go to great lengths to suck you back into the relationship. With an overt, grandiose narcissist, this might look like an apology using a grand gesture such as an expensive gift or an over-the-top display of affection or a last-minute trip away. With a covert, vulnerable narcissist, they may be more helpful around the house or do things they know you'll approve of that validate they are a good partner and a good person. It may also involve the future faking, baiting, and manipulative memory recall that I mentioned previously. This phase leads right back into the idealization phase and, often, these two phases seemingly blend into one another as the relationship continues over time.

Advice: Pay attention to *how* the narcissist apologizes. Do they truly take accountability for their actions and the hurt they caused? Or are they only apologizing merely to smooth things over, while still shifting the blame onto you? Perhaps they don't apologize at all, sweeping everything under the rug. This might leave you feeling slightly relieved, initially, but later, unsettled, as the underlying issues remain unresolved.

An overt, grandiose narcissist may rely on a grand gesture as a distraction, expecting it to be enough without addressing the harm they caused or taking accountability. A covert, vulnerable narcissist may apologize but deflect responsibility, blaming external factors, like stress, work, or even you, for their behavior. In both cases, the apology often lacks genuine empathy or understanding of how much they've hurt you.

This superficial approach to apologizing leaves you feeling unheard, unseen, unimportant, and misunderstood, with no meaningful effort made to change their hurtful behaviors. True accountability and understanding will always be missing in these interactions, keeping the cycle of manipulation intact.

Further Reflection on the Narcissistic Abuse Cycle

With regards to the length of the narcissistic abuse cycles, do overt narcissists complete the abuse cycle once in a shorter-term relationship whereas covert narcissists repeat the cycle over and over and over again, lasting for many years, even decades? While I have not studied a huge sample of data for decades on the behavioral patterns of narcissists, it has been my experience that more often than not, we observe that the overt, grandiose narcissist may have a string of short-term relationships where this cycle plays out in entirety once to a few times, whereas a covert, vulnerable narcissist may repeat this cycle multiple times over many, many years in long-term relationships without being detected due to the subtle nature of how they operate.

Now, let's read Michelle's story and see if you can identify the different cycles of abuse and the different patterns of behavior and tactics used in each phase. Please note that this story is completely fictional; however, it draws upon real-life examples from my own life and others. Don't worry, I'll make it easy for you as I'll be pointing out the truth of what's really going on throughout the story, and the chapter headings will clue you in as well!

Part Two

A Tale of Narcissistic Abuse

Chapter Four

IDEALIZATION—THE BEGINNING

Michelle grew up in a suburb of Boston with dreams of becoming a high-powered career woman. She remembered stomping around her childhood home wearing her mother's high heels, red lipstick all over her face, and her hair messily pulled back into a chignon.

She couldn't wait to grow up and become a powerful, successful executive—an idea that her mother reinforced throughout her childhood with comments about how Michelle would one day become financially independent and highly successful. She loved that Michelle always seemed to know what she wanted from such a young age, without realizing that those ideas were actually seeded subconsciously by her. As a child, Michelle was very bright, highly motivated, ultra-determined, and always well-mannered, which persisted as she matured. She also had people-pleasing tendencies and identified as a perfectionist, afraid to disappoint or offend anyone at the risk of being disliked or rejected. It's what drove her to excel in both her academic and professional pursuits.

Those qualities—her determination, perfectionism, and deep desire to succeed—propelled her into the high-powered career she had always dreamed of, and now she found herself on the brink of achieving it. After weeks of rigorous interviews, Michelle felt she was finally on the verge of securing an offer for her dream job, a culmination of her years of hard work and relentless ambition.

During her final interview, she met with Mike. The interview went really well, and he seemed to like her. The conversation had gone smoothly. He asked her many questions which she answered with ease, proving her value and ability to be a team player. She explained how her depth of experience could fill the gaps on his current team. Mike seemed to be impressed with Michelle, and they discovered during the interview that they had many things in common. It turned out that, despite their age difference, they had similar professional experiences and had worked for the same company in previous iterations of their careers on the same floor. They had just never met. Michelle walked away feeling confident the job would be hers.

Less than twenty-four hours later, she received the phone call she had been expecting, and when she was told she would be reporting directly to Mike, she was glad. Out of everyone she had met, she felt they had hit it off best and felt most at ease with him, in a professional sense, of course. After all, Mike was married, and Michelle was not about to mix business with pleasure again; she had made that mistake before. She certainly would never cross the line with her boss, even if he was handsome.

On her first day, Michelle arrived excited and eager to begin getting to know the team and learning how things worked at her new firm. When Mike arrived shortly after Michelle, he smiled at her, welcomed her to the firm, and said, "I'm really glad we hired you instead of Brad. You're much prettier!"

At first, Michelle was taken aback, but then she laughed it off nervously because a part of her was flattered that her good-looking boss thought she was pretty. On the other hand, she felt uncomfortable and nervously looked around to see if anyone else thought it was inappropriate. She wasn't exactly about to go running to HR to tell them her new boss had just hit on her when she had been dreaming of working for this firm for as long as she could remember.

It had taken her a long time to get here. She wasn't about to blow it all up for an offhand comment made by her boss, who she already could tell was very charming. No one else seemed to flinch, so she decided to let it go, figuring she was overreacting.

Months went by, and Mike never made another comment about how pretty Michelle was again. Occasionally he would tell her he liked her shoes or that a certain color suited her, but that was it. She settled into her new work environment and was glad to work with Mike and the team.

The holidays were approaching, and the team was working on a big deal. It required all hands on deck. The problem was that Mike had a vacation planned, so he asked Michelle to be the front-runner on the project, to be his right-hand woman. Michelle was flattered that Mike had trusted her enough to lead the deal when she had been with the firm for fewer than six months. Either way, she took it as a sign she was doing well and he trusted her with the responsibility. Secretly, she thought it was a good sign because bonus season was coming up.

Before Mike headed out of the office for a two-week holiday overseas, he asked Michelle for her mobile number, and he gave her his so they could continue to communicate about the deal while he was away. Yes, he was trusting her to take the reins while he was gone; however, he knew she would need guidance, and he asked to be kept in the loop every step of the way.

Initially, Mike called to check in at least once a day to ask how things were going. Michelle would update him on their progress, and he would provide direction and guidance. The phone calls at this point were mostly during business hours, which was tough since Mike was vacationing in a different time zone. Soon, the phone calls began to come in at all hours of the day—early morning, late evening, and rarely during the middle of the day.

Michelle asked Mike, "Are you enjoying your vacation at all? You seem to never sleep!" Mike replied that he was trying to make the calls while his family was otherwise engaged so they didn't know how much he was still working while on vacation, something that would've frustrated his family.

Quietly, Mike admitted, "You know, my wife would actually be really upset if she knew how much we were talking."

Michelle couldn't understand why. They weren't doing anything wrong. He had made it sound like they were doing something inappropriate, when it was all very innocent and only about work.

Defensively, she said, "But we are talking about work, nothing more. Why would she be upset? Because you're working too much?"

He replied, "Well, yes, she would be upset that I was working this much, but she'd be even more annoyed if she knew I was speaking with you. She doesn't like it when I speak to other women, especially beautiful, smart, younger women. Hell, she doesn't even like it when I speak to my assistant, Helen, and she's twice your age! I guess you could say she's a little insecure. It may surprise you to know that not everyone is as confident and secure as you, Michelle."

"Uhmmmm...?" Michelle stammered. She wasn't exactly sure which comment she found more incredulous—the comment about being a beautiful, smart, younger woman or the comment about being confident and secure. "Okay, I guess. I feel bad for her. That's an awful way for your wife to feel."

"Yes, I agree. She worries about everything. She's a worry wart. It can be a bit exhausting, to be honest. And hold on a second, did you just say you guess? Are you the type of woman who can't accept a compliment? Because honestly, you should be comfortable with the truth," Mike said, as if discounting his wife's feelings and changing the subject.

When Michelle hung up the phone, she felt bad for Lucy, Mike's wife. She empathized with her anxiety. After all, Michelle had struggled with anxiety on and off throughout her life, so she could understand perhaps why Lucy would have a fear of abandonment or losing her closest loved ones. (Michelle was very empathetic.)

On the other hand, Michelle was in shock that her boss was so upfront and assertive. Yes, he was like that in the office, but Michelle felt like he was being extremely flirtatious with her, leaving her feeling both uncomfortable and deeply flattered. It had been a while since a man flirted with Michelle. She spent most of her time at work, so it didn't leave much time to have a life outside of the office.

Her last relationship was part of the reason she was looking for a new job when she did. That relationship had gone up in flames, and the worst part was that it all blew up at the office holiday party in front of her colleagues. Michelle had been dating an associate who worked in another department, and they had been really good at keeping things under wraps—until she found him kissing her boss's secretary in the coat check at the ultra-chic holiday party after the cocktail hour. Michelle was usually much more composed and never one to cause a scene. However, that day, she had skipped lunch to get her hair blown out for the party and had had a few drinks on an empty stomach during the cocktail hour. She totally lost it when, completely by accident, she found the two of them in the coat check!

Needless to say, she had been eager to find a new job after that. She couldn't bear the embarrassment and all the whispers about her behavior after the fact.

* * *

The next day, Mike called her at two o'clock in the morning to check in. Michelle had been in a deep sleep, and she didn't realize it was her phone ringing.

When she saw his name show up on the screen of her phone, she groaned. She was so tired. The last thing she felt like doing was answering the phone and talking about work in the middle of the night.

"Hello," Michelle answered with a husky voice that surprised even her.

"Hey Michelle, wow! You sound like you smoked a pack of cigarettes. I'm sorry for waking you. I wanted to check in before we head out for the day for an excursion."

"Sure," Michelle responded. "Just give me a minute to wake up."

"No problem. How are things going? Were you able to connect with John to go over everything before we finalize the details?" Mike asked.

"Uhh... Yes. I did. I spoke to him yesterday afternoon. Are you enjoying your trip? Hope you're headed somewhere fun today."

"Yes, we are going on a tour of some ancient ruins, and then we are taking a private cooking class as a family at a nearby olive grove," Mike responded, sounding very unenthused.

"That sounds amazing! Shouldn't you be more excited?" Michelle asked. If she didn't know any better, she would have thought he was depressed.

Mike sighed. Michelle imagined him running his hands through his hair as he sighed.

"To be honest, I think I am going to need a vacation from this vacation. Things with Lucy and me are tenuous, at best. I'm not sure we are going to survive this trip, forget about a lifetime. We fight over everything. To be honest, this trip was planned as a last-ditch effort to try to save our marriage. I'm just not sure it's going to work. I don't know what to do. I can't imagine not being with my kids; however, I also can't imagine continuing to live with constant hostility and resentment either. Ughhh!"

Michelle wasn't quite sure how to respond. On one hand, she couldn't believe how open and honest Mike was being about his relationship. On the other hand, she didn't want to brush him off and embarrass him. She empathized with his situation. After all, her own parents had gotten divorced when she was in junior high. Michelle couldn't understand Mike's fear of not being able to see his kids if he got a divorce. Surely, his wife wouldn't keep his kids from him, even if it was as bad as Mike made it sound.

"Why wouldn't you get to see your kids if you two got divorced? Wouldn't Lucy want you to spend time with them?" Michelle asked. "You have rights as their father too, you know."

Mike didn't even hesitate in his response. "I just know that if we get divorced, she's going to poison them against me, and she's going to make it very difficult for me to see them. After all, I work really long hours, so if I'm lucky, I'll get them every other weekend. I can't even fathom that!" he said disdainfully. Clearing his throat and regaining his composure, Mike continued, "Anyway, I am sorry. I don't know why I am sharing all of this with you. Let's finish catching up on work so you can get back to bed."

After Michelle hung up the phone, she had trouble falling asleep. She felt bad for Mike and wished there was something she could do, while at the same time she felt honored that he felt comfortable enough opening up to her. Being stuck inside an unhealthy marriage for the sake of your kids was not something Michelle could relate to; she'd never been married, nor did she have kids. Regardless, she felt bad for him and the difficult situation he was in.

When her parents got divorced, she was in junior high. Yes, it had been tough to adjust to the transition, but overall, she was grateful they had separated. At least she didn't have to hear her parents fighting or feel the tension in the air when they faked being happy for the sake of other people when they were out in public. It was humiliating to watch them be fake with one another when everyone else knew they hated each other.

Michelle reasoned that the kids would be fine if Mike and his wife got divorced; she just wasn't sure if Mike would be okay. Maybe she could convince him by sharing her experience as a child of divorced parents and show him that while it would be an adjustment, being happy and less stressed would be better overall for his kids! Plus, they would get his undivided attention when they were with him. That was one thing Michelle loved after her parents divorced. She got quality time with each of them, individually. It was better than being with two unhappy parents who traded passive-aggressive insults at each other all day long.

* * *

Just as they were wrapping up the deal, Mike returned from vacation. He thanked Michelle publicly for her hard work and for carrying the team while he was away. It was such a public display of gratitude in front of the whole team that Michelle blushed with embarrassment. Michelle realized she really *was* bad at accepting a compliment. She decided she'd have to work on that. She hated it when she watched her mother resist the compliments of other men once she started dating again, because it always seemed like she was fishing for reassurance or another compliment. That's not who she wanted to become!

Later that evening, she received a text message from Mike.

"Hey! Are you home?"

"Yes. Is everything okay? Do you need me to come back to the office?" Michelle replied.

The three dots appeared, and it seemed to be taking Mike a while to respond. A part of her was apprehensive, and yet another part was curiously excited to hear from him. She wondered if she should just call him because the waiting was kind of killing her.

During one of their late-night texts, while Mike was away, he told her that she was on track to receive a promotion soon if she kept up the good work. He also began opening up more about his childhood, especially after she shared her experience of growing up with divorced parents and how it was so much better to have two happy parents in two homes than two miserable parents in one. To her surprise, his parents had also divorced when he was even younger than Michelle. His mom was mentally and emotionally unstable, and it took a toll on Mike. Michelle felt a deep empathy for that wounded little boy who never felt safe or truly loved by his mother.

Mike had also shared in more detail how he and Lucy had been at each other's throats for months, if not years, and how the strains began years ago after they had children. He felt like his kids had replaced him and that his wife was no longer affectionate with him. He spent nights alone while she fell asleep in their youngest daughter's room.

There were other problems too. It wasn't just that his wife was insecure about Mike talking to other women, but rather that she didn't trust him at all. Michelle had asked if he had ever cheated on her. It seemed strange to her that she didn't trust him at all, especially since she married him! He swore up and down he never ever cheated on Lucy, and he wasn't that type of guy.

Michelle felt sorry for Mike, his wife, and his children. She couldn't understand how his wife couldn't see what a great guy Mike was and that inside he was just a little boy who wanted to feel loved and accepted. Michelle wished she could help, which she knew was crazy because it wasn't her place. All she could do was listen and encourage him to be honest with Lucy about how he felt. He claimed he had tried in the past to have open conversations with her about how he felt, but Lucy always seemed to find a way to turn things around on him and make him out to be the bad guy. No matter how many times he tried to communicate with her, she always made herself out to be the victim. "Apparently," he said, "nothing I did was ever good enough or right in her eyes. Ever."

"Hahaha!" Michelle laughed, trying to make light of the situation. "I'm sure that's not entirely true. I can't imagine your wife truly feels that way."

Mike assured her that it was absolutely true and explained that Lucy always made him the scapegoat of all of their relationship issues, and as a result, Mike was constantly just trying to placate her to keep the peace.

It sounded to Michelle like Lucy's head and heart were no longer in the marriage. Michelle couldn't imagine a relationship, never mind a marriage, where a wife could be so indifferent and cold toward her husband. Maybe *she* was cheating on Mike? *No, no, no. That was a crazy thought,* Michelle scolded herself silently.

Mike really seemed like a wounded bird during these conversations, which was so unlike the version of him she had witnessed in the office. At work, he was confident, strong, determined, funny, and always in a good mood. In these private conversations, he sounded so defeated, insecure, sensitive, and—could she admit—fragile?!

Deep within, Michelle realized it probably wasn't appropriate for Mike to divulge this information about his private life, but she wasn't sure how to end these conversations without seeming rude or insensitive. To be fair, most of the confessions began during the middle of the night when Mike was on vacation overseas and she was half asleep. She figured it was easier at the time to let him talk freely rather than being rude and curt and upsetting him more. After all, she didn't want to brush him off and risk getting the cold shoulder. He had entrusted her to run this massive deal at work in his absence. Plus, he had told her in confidence she was getting noticed by other senior partners in the firm for how well she was handling things.

A part of her didn't want to muck things up and possibly miss out on the promotion or, even worse, lose her job!

Michelle had asked if Mike had any friends he could talk to about his marriage. He explained that his guy friends wouldn't understand what he was going through, and they would probably make fun of him for being so sensitive.

Geesh, Michelle thought, *guys can be so full of machismo sometimes.* It sounded to her like Mike needed a better set of friends!

Mike said he knew it probably was not appropriate to share all this personal information with her, but he really had no one else to talk to. He told her he knew he could trust her, she had proven that already, and he felt safe sharing with her because he knew she would be discreet.

"Besides," Mike said, "I know you wouldn't want to be the talk of the office by being seen as the boss's pet or, God forbid, have people think we were sleeping together!"

Michelle had turned a bright crimson red and started sweating at the latter part of his statement. *Would people really think we were sleeping together? My reputation would be destroyed; I'd lose my job.* (He was playing on Michelle's empathy and maintaining his power in the relationship—this also was a way of making sure that Michelle wouldn't share this with anyone because she would risk her promotion and/or job. Plus, Mike now knew that she was roped in by her empathy and fear.)

Michelle's phone finally chirped, pulling her out of her reverie of recalling past conversations.

"I have something I need to drop off to you. What's your address?"

Confused, she responded, "Okay, sure. My address is 384 W. 74th Street, Apt. 4B."

Michelle wasn't sure how she felt about Mike stopping by. Yes, they'd become friends, but he was still her boss. Michelle shook her head and silently said to herself, *He's just dropping something off; he's not coming inside.* She decided that when he arrived, she would meet him out in the hallway after the doorman called to announce his arrival, just to be safe. She didn't want to create any awkward situations.

Fifteen minutes later, Mike was getting off the elevator and walking down the long hallway toward her apartment. Michelle was standing outside the door watching him as he approached, and he had this sheepish grin on his face. If Michelle was honest with herself, that grin was making her stomach do funny things.

"Hi," Mike said, "I'm glad you were home. I just happened to be in the neighborhood."

Michelle laughed. She knew Mike had no business being in her neighborhood. He lived on the opposite side of town.

Now that he'd broken the ice, Mike handed her a box that was wrapped with a gorgeous red ribbon, along with a card. The box looked almost like it was a jewelry box containing a bracelet or a watch. Michelle was confused and hesitantly took the box.

Mike immediately picked up on her discomfort and said, "It's not what it looks like. I just wanted to thank you for taking the reins while I was out of the office trying to figure everything out with my family. And... for being such a good friend. You're a really good listener!" With that, he touched her shoulder and kissed her on the side of the head.

Michelle noticed how good he smelled. She felt electricity run down her shoulder where he touched her, and her right temple was burning hot after he kissed it. She was confused by what she was feeling. He's her boss, and he probably shouldn't be here.

He noticed she seemed to be holding her breath and quickly said, "I'm sorry for dropping in on you like this so last minute. I didn't think it was appropriate to give you this in the office. Everyone would think I was playing favorites, and I'm sure HR would frown upon it. I promise it's nothing exciting, so don't get your hopes up. You can open it later if you'd like."

"No, no. Don't be silly. I really appreciate the gesture. It's very kind, although completely unnecessary." Michelle slowly unwrapped the gift, and when she finally got the box opened, she saw it was a very expensive fountain pen. She was stunned. *How in the world did Mike know she had a thing for fountain pens?* In their late-night talks, she was pretty sure she never mentioned she and her father had shared a love of fountain pens.

Again, Mike noticed the swirl of emotions on Michelle's face and said, "You think I'm not paying attention, but I pay attention to the people I care about. I noticed that you always seem to write with a fountain pen during our meetings. I know nothing about them, so I asked a friend of mine who collects them to help me pick it out."

Wow! Michelle had *no* idea that Mike cared or noticed her enough to be aware of something as simple as what kind of pen she writes with. She found this oddly endearing. Her heart was starting to melt a little. No one had ever paid that much attention to her before, not even her last serious, dipshit boyfriend. She had been lucky if the guys she was dating noticed what color her eyes were—forget about noticing something with so much sentimental meaning. Her father had passed the year before, so using one of his fountain pens every day made her feel like he was still with her. She started to cry.

Mike was not expecting that reaction and started to panic, thinking she didn't like his gift. He started apologizing, saying that he thought he had done a good thing and how his wife must be right—he never did or said the right thing. His shoulders slumped forward, and his head hung down between them.

Shocked, Michelle pulled herself together when she saw that she had hurt Mike's feelings and started comforting him. (She was ignoring how she felt to focus on Mike's feelings instead, as she likely learned as a child that her emotions were not important or not as important as other people's.)

They found themselves hugging in the middle of the hallway as she thanked him for the gift and apologized for getting so emotional. At the same time, Mike apologized for trying to do something nice that caused her to get upset.

Immediately, Michelle pulled away from the embrace and looked at Mike, full of compassion. She couldn't imagine how anyone could think Mike was a not a good guy. She began to say how it was the most thoughtful gift anyone had ever given her when he stopped her in her tracks by asking, "Can I hug you a little longer? It felt so nice to hug you."

Michelle's heart went out to Mike. She quietly said, "Yes." After all, she hadn't been hugged like that, perhaps, ever in her life. They hugged a little longer and Michelle was overcome with this weird, tingly feeling she'd never experienced before.

A minute later, Mike's phone started ringing. He groaned, "It's Lucy."

Upon hearing Lucy's name, Michelle snapped back to reality and quickly thanked Mike for the very thoughtful gift. Her face flushed, and she abruptly turned and headed back into the safe confines of her apartment as Mike stared blankly at the screen on his phone and headed down the hallway to the elevator to take the call.

Confused and flustered, Michelle closed the door and slumped down onto the floor. She wasn't sure what had just happened, how it happened, or why she felt this weird tingling feeling and warmth spreading across her chest. She felt guilty for some reason, and she was not sure why. She felt responsible for making Mike feel bad when he was trying to do something nice. Michelle also felt guilty for hugging Mike just before his wife called him.

She knew it was innocent and there was nothing sexual about it; she was just comforting a friend whose feelings she had hurt. (Here, Michelle was taking accountability for something that wasn't her responsibility, and while she was emotional not *because* of Mike, he made it all about him by becoming the victim. This was the way he manipulated her into giving him a hug. He was slowly pushing her boundaries, but he was doing it in a way that was below Michelle's level of awareness. He would continue to push until he got what he wanted or needed from her.)

Michelle pulled out her phone and tapped a quick text to Mike, "Thank you again for the very thoughtful gift. My father loved fountain pens, so they are very special to me. I really appreciate it, and I'm sorry if you thought you did something wrong when you were trying to do something nice. Enjoy the rest of your evening."

Mike didn't respond. Michelle didn't expect him to. She knew he was now rushing home to be with his family. She just couldn't have him thinking he did anything wrong. (Once again, she took responsibility for his emotions, focusing on making him feel better while overlooking any potential red flags in how he asked to hug her longer.)

* * *

Weeks went by. Michelle and Mike continued their friendship, which remained completely platonic aside from the fact that when they were alone, they chatted about their personal lives. Michelle began offering Mike advice because she felt bad that he was in a tough situation. He told her he valued her advice because she was a woman and likely understood his wife better than he did. Michelle laughed at that because there was no way she could understand how Lucy could not see what a kind, sensitive man Mike was and how much he cared about her and their children. (He's positioned himself as the good guy and the victim and his wife as the difficult, insecure, and harsh perpetrator.)

One day, after work, as they were riding the elevator down together to the lobby, Mike asked Michelle what she was doing after work. She mentioned that she was going to a yoga class with a friend not far from the office. They ended up walking together for a couple of blocks before parting ways. As they were about to say goodbye, Mike said, "I think it's great how well you take care of your body. You're in great shape. I wish my wife would care about herself as much as you do. I know you'll never let yourself go like she has. Enjoy your class! See you tomorrow!" (Planting a seed.)

Michelle said goodbye and headed toward her friend, who was waiting for her across the street outside the studio. Her friend asked who that handsome, older gentleman was! Michelle blushed and said, "My boss, and back off, he's married!" They laughed as they entered the studio.

As the weeks went by, Michelle noticed that she cared more and more about how she looked when she went to work. She began to seek Mike out to ask questions and check in. They began spending more and more time together, grabbing coffee together or finding reasons to work more closely together on various projects.

One evening, while the two of them were working late on a project alone, Mike mentioned how the office felt so different at night when no one else was around. Michelle agreed. The office felt like their safe space to spend time together without worrying about the judgment of their coworkers. (Creating a sense of safety.)

Mike proceeded to tell Michelle he was pretty sure that a guy on their team, Kevin, was attracted to her, and that, as a guy, he could tell. Michelle started laughing. "Stop. That's absurd. Linda, who sits right next to Kevin, is much more attractive. I'm pretty sure he has a crush on her, not me."

Mike looks at her bewildered, then he sighed and ran his fingers through his hair.

"What?" she said.

Shaking his head, he said, "You think Linda is more attractive than you? Why would you think that? She doesn't have your eyes, your body, your intelligence, or your personality! You are definitely way more attractive than Linda."

Michelle, who was never at a loss for words, felt her breath catch in the back of her throat. The wheels in her head were turning. Mike thought she was more attractive than Linda?! Linda was supermodel material; how could that be?

"You seriously don't know how sexy you are, do you? I bet you don't even notice how many heads turn when you walk down the hallway either, do you?"

Again, Michelle didn't know how to respond. Of course she didn't notice. Michelle had always felt like the ugly duckling of her family. There was nothing special about her. Well, except her hair. She'd always loved her hair, as long as it wasn't humid outside.

Mike interrupted her thoughts and said, "You're so sexy, I could kiss you right now."

Whoa! Michelle felt lightheaded. She was spinning. *What did he just say? Did she hear him correctly? He couldn't have possibly said that. Could he?*

Her handsome boss and friend who was kind, sensitive, and thoughtful was telling her he thought she was not just attractive but also sexy. And he wanted to kiss her?! It was too much for her brain to comprehend. She just kept shaking her head in protest, trying to shake off the compliments that felt too big to accept.

Michelle was exhausted. They had spent the last couple of weeks working really late to complete the project they were working on before the deadline the next morning. Maybe that was why she was having a hard time processing what was happening or believing what she heard. As a matter of fact, she was pretty sure she was imagining this whole scenario in some sort of delirious daydream.

Next thing she knew, however, Mike had crossed the room and was standing in front of her, only inches away, quietly asking her if he could kiss her. Michelle could feel the heat emanating from him. He smelled so good. There was a look in his eyes she couldn't quite make sense of. She felt as though she could see the little boy inside of him asking her for acceptance.

She started to back away and said, "I'm not sure. I don't think that would be a good idea. You're married and my boss."

He quickly paced back to the other side of the room, his breathing sharp and erratic, as he grew visibly upset.

"You know what I've been through. You know how hard I've tried to fix my marriage. I'm not happy. She's not happy. We fight all of the time. My kids are miserable. My marriage is over." (Making excuses to make her feel safe in this situation and justify his behavior.)

He rushed back toward her, took her hands in his, and said, "You. You are the one who understands me. You're the one who gets me. She doesn't. And I think I know you pretty well too. In fact, I probably know you better than you know yourself. I know you feel something when we're together because I feel it too. When I'm with her, I feel nothing. We are just roommates going through the motions. I have so much love to give and no one to give it to." (Playing on her empathy again.)

Michelle couldn't deny what he had just said. He did know her better than most people, and she did feel a closeness between them. She also felt sorry for him. She could see the little boy inside who was suffering. She leaned forward and put her arms around him. So, when he started to pull away shortly after, she leaned back into him to stay locked in the embrace for a little while longer. She wanted him to know that she understood and cared for him.

She felt like she needed more time to sort through her emotions and her thoughts. Mike was right. She felt seen and cared for like she never had before. Mike seemed to see right through her. He did know her better than she knew herself, and here he was, wanting to kiss her. Mike knew her for who she was and didn't run off in the opposite direction like so many of her exes before him had. Rather, he was asking her to kiss him.

He could see the turmoil in her eyes but when he gently lowered his lips to hers, she didn't stop him. The kiss was unlike anything she had ever felt before. Michelle lost herself inside that kiss. It seemed to fill the gaping holes left in her heart after years of disappointing relationships where she never felt seen, heard, loved, respected, or understood.

When Mike pulled away, he began stroking Michelle's hair away from her face as Michelle put her hand over her mouth. She instantly felt guilty. She felt conflicted. She felt tears sting the back of her eyes. She didn't know what to say. Mike, however, did.

"Wow. Just wow! That was beyond anything I could have ever imagined." Then he saw the look on her face and that she was on the verge of tears. "Are you okay? Please don't feel guilty. I told you. My marriage is over. There is no love between us anymore."

In the awkward pause, Michelle nodded her head as though she understood. Mike pulled out his phone, looked at his text messages and said, "It's late. We should go home, and Lucy is apparently wondering where I am."

Michelle became overwhelmed with anguish. She didn't want Mike to see it, so she pretended she was okay as he jogged toward the elevator bank.

She was beginning to hate seeing him run toward elevator bank to go home and see his wife. Ugh!

Later that evening, as Michelle tried to fall asleep, all she could think about was how, if she felt this guilty about something that felt so good, then she imagined Mike must be struggling even more. She thought about texting him to ask if he was okay, but she needed some space to gather her thoughts.

Reflections

In this first stage of the abuse cycle, we witnessed the tactic of grooming. During Mike and Michelle's first interaction, Mike was trying to establish a foundation of familiarity by identifying people they knew in common or their similar work experiences. Later on, he went on to share about how he and his wife were on the verge of getting divorced, which may or may not have been true. Then he tested Michelle's boundaries by reaching out to her after work hours, sharing personal information, and testing the limits of her empathy. With regards to how empathetic Michelle was, Mike was able to see how easily he could manipulate her into feeling for him and how responsible she may or may not feel for trying to fix or help him with his crumbling marriage (codependent traits). He also benefited from Michelle's ability to easily make excuses for his inappropriate behavior. This foundation of familiarity, combined with Mike's false truths, Michelle's deep empathy, naivete, and lack of boundaries, paved the way for Mike's ability to manipulate Michelle into crossing the boundaries of their professional relationship and excusing his inappropriate advances.

We also saw that Mike love bombed Michelle by giving her inappropriate compliments, gifting her the pen, paying extra attention to her, and trying to win her over with his charm.

He began to lay it on thick when they spent the evening working late at the office. He tried to play it off as though he was jealous that their coworker Kevin had a crush on Michelle. He recognized that she didn't see herself as attractive or at least not as attractive as their coworker Linda. That was when Mike swooped in and love bombed her, and in her confusion and his flattery, he kissed her. It was the moment when things begin to pivot in their relationship.

We are also beginning to see the emergence of other tactics which we will address at the end of the next chapter.

Chapter Five

Devaluation and Discard—The Abuse

The next few days at work, Michelle felt like a zombie just going through the motions. She wasn't sleeping at night. She still felt so conflicted. She and Mike hadn't really spoken outside of the office about what had happened. As a matter of fact, it felt as if he was avoiding her.

She was confused. He was the one who had initiated the whole thing. Why did she feel so triggered? It's not like he was dumping her. They weren't even a thing. Maybe it was because he had lit the match and then walked away, leaving everything else to burn and crumble around her. She felt overwhelmed, like she was slowly drowning in confusion and other conflicting emotions. It was torture not knowing how he felt. (Her attachment wounds are coming up.)

Did she have feelings for Mike? Yes, perhaps, but it was hard to discern because the guilt and shame overshadowed how she felt. She wanted to be near Mike and yet, nowhere near him. She wanted to be comforted by him, and yet she knew that was a bad idea. It felt dangerous to be around him, but they had to work together and pretend everything was fine.

She hadn't realized she was staring in his direction as all these thoughts passed through her mind. He saw her staring and gave her a little smile. She felt a pang in her chest. He had been ignoring her for days. He didn't even respond to her text when she asked the next day if he was okay. She was worried about him because if she was feeling as guilty as she was, he must be feeling even more guilty.

That little smile, however, said otherwise. It was almost a mischievous smile as if they had a secret between them, which of course, she guessed they did. Ugh.

That afternoon, she decided to head out to grab a coffee. She was exhausted and still had to get through at least four more hours of work. Just as the elevator doors were about to close, a hand stopped them. There standing before her was Mike. She had been alone in the elevator, and she gasped when he nearly lost his hand trying to stop the elevator to get on.

As they rode down to the lobby, he turned to her and said, "Hey, how are you?"

"Fine, I guess. I texted you the other day, but you never responded. Are you okay?"

Quickly, he replied, "Look, we don't have a lot of time, but I need this to stop. It's too much for me. I'm trying to figure things out with Lucy. She's the mother of my children. I can't just screw up my marriage for a hot, young thing from the office."

Michelle felt like she had just taken a punch to the gut. She was literally stunned into silence, trying to gasp for air. *What did he just say? Where was this coming from? Why was he turning this on her? He was the one who said his marriage was over. He was the one who initiated the kiss and then told her not to feel guilty afterward. Now, he's working on his marriage?* So many thoughts flooded her brain that she wasn't sure which one to verbalize first!

Just as she had finally composed herself and was about to respond, the elevator doors flew open, and he walked out.

She couldn't believe what had happened. She walked quickly after him, following him, and when she caught up, she quietly said under her breath, "Please, we need to talk about this. This wasn't my fault. I didn't start this."

He turned on his heel, looked her square in the eye and said, "You sure as hell didn't. You walk around here dressed the way you do, looking at me with those puppy-dog eyes. How is this all my fault? You took advantage of me when I was weak and vulnerable. You knew I was struggling and emotional. You saw your chance, and you took it. How can I work with you day in and day out now? I'll constantly be reminded of what happened, and the guilt will eat me alive." With that, he stormed off.

Michelle just stood there. Her mind was spinning in circles. Where was this coming from? *Was it* all her fault? Did she take advantage? She knew he had been struggling and that he hadn't felt loved or appreciated at home. *Did she* reveal how she felt without knowing it? Could he tell when she had begun to fall for him? She began to question everything. She replayed the weeks leading up to this moment, trying to identify if she had been leading him on or if she had been flirtatious unknowingly. She felt ashamed, but at the same time, she felt confused, irritated, and hurt. (Mike was using DARVO, making Michelle the offender and himself the victim.)

Michelle had moved to *this* city for *this* job. Her friends back home didn't know anything about her new life. She was never very good at keeping in touch. She couldn't possibly call up one of her friends from back home to help her process what had happened because that meant catching them up on the last ten months *and* admitting that she had kissed a married man. And not just any married man, but her *boss*!? She began to question who she was. This was so out of character for her. No one would even believe it! She could barely believe it had happened, not to mention the events that just occurred.

She decided to get some fresh air to clear her head. Michelle walked around the block as she tried to unpack what had just happened. A part of her could see Mike was struggling. He was scared. He was afraid of breaking up his family because of his kids. He was afraid of being labeled the bad guy, yet again. He had told her as much. Maybe he was just freaked out.

Plus, they had been so exhausted after working so many late nights together; maybe he misremembered what had happened, or maybe Michelle had been more suggestive or too flirtatious when they were together. Sure, they joked around; they swapped stories about bad relationships. He knew her better than she knew herself, so maybe she was putting out kiss-me vibes and didn't realize it. (The poison seed Mike had planted was now being watered by Michelle. She believed Mike knew her better than she knew herself so she believed that perhaps he was right and she instigated the kiss.)

When Michelle returned to her desk, she tried as hard as she could to throw herself into her work. Thankfully, it was Friday, so she wouldn't have to see Mike until Monday. Secretly, she hoped to hear from him to clear the air. Knowing how angry he was made her uncomfortable. She always hated it when someone was upset with her, but now there was this added complication that he was also her boss.

She couldn't imagine what would happen on Monday morning when she walked into the office. Would he continue to ignore her? Smile at her again? Would she have to continue to walk on eggshells until he calmed down or would he blow up at her again? All she knew was that she was going to keep her distance for now because as much as she wanted to apologize for what had happened, she also didn't want to set him off again like she had earlier. (Notice Michelle was taking responsibility; she felt accountable like she had to walk on eggshells.)

Monday came and went. So did Tuesday, Wednesday, and Thursday! Michelle kept her head down and focused on her work while remaining hypervigilant of Mike's every move. It was distracting to say the least.

Mike, for the most part, ignored her. He wouldn't even look her in the eye, and if he had to speak to her, it was by speaking in her general direction without actually addressing her. (Silent treatment.)

Michelle didn't know what to make of it, but it was exhausting. She felt like she was on high alert at all times, constantly aware of his every move, word, and action. She didn't know if he was still mad and would blow up at her the next time he caught her alone, or if he would apologize and try to make amends.

Michelle tried to stay busy. She felt paranoid, constantly looking over her shoulder to see if he had followed her when she left to get lunch, go to the bathroom, or grab a coffee. She didn't want to get blindsided again, but she also wanted—no needed—to talk to him. All of this was making her feel a little insane!

Finally, it was early Friday morning. As Michelle took the elevator up to her floor, she kept repeating to herself under her breath, "You just have to get through today, and then it's the weekend. Just one more day... one more day.... You've got this, Michelle!"

By the time she stepped off the elevator, she had psyched herself up and convinced herself it would be easier to get a head start on her work while it was quiet and before everyone else arrived for the day. It also helped that she wouldn't be distracted by Mike's presence for at least another hour or so.

By the time he arrived in the office, she had finished her coffee and was in a groove, working and tackling the things she had to get done for the latest deal they were working on.

As he walked past her desk, Mike unexpectedly handed her a note and said good morning. He seemed to be in a good mood. He didn't appear to be angry. She figured that was a good thing.

Before she opened the note, she quickly glanced around to make sure no one else had noticed. Once she saw she was in the clear, she opened the envelope and read: "Meet me at the coffee shop across the street at 10:00 a.m. We need to talk."

Michelle felt a wave of anxiety. She was glad he was no longer freezing her out, but she had no clue what was going through his mind. The last she had heard from him, he seemed to blame her for everything. She wasn't sure if she would be walking into an apology or firing squad.

To make matters worse, she felt like she was coming down with something. She had felt horrible all week. She could barely sleep or eat, she felt like she was battling a never-ending headache behind her eyes, and her throat was starting to hurt.

At the same time, however, with each day that passed without a single word from him, she felt anger rising beneath the surface. How could he give her the silent treatment all week, especially when he admitted that he cared about her? Or maybe he didn't? Maybe she wasn't remembering what had happened accurately. She was confused.

She had spent hours looking in the mirror, planning what she would say to him when he finally spoke to her. Now she couldn't remember any of it. Maybe she would just let him do the talking.

Just before 10:00, Michelle made her way to the coffee shop feeling nervous, excited, and angry all at the same time.

When she opened the door to the coffee shop, she took a deep breath to settle her anxiety as she spotted him sitting at a table in the back. He was nervously straightening his shirt, so he didn't see her, but one look at him and her anger melted away. He looked about as nervous and hesitant as she felt. What if one of their colleagues saw them chatting together at the coffee shop, when they could have just ducked into a conference room in the office?

Feeling self-conscious as she walked by the tables of the other patrons, she kept focusing on her breathing.

"Hello," Michelle said as she quickly sat down across from him.

"Hi," Mike replied, "Thank you for meeting me. I wasn't sure if you would come or not."

"Well, it was nice of you to finally reach out after nearly a week of the silent treatment following your outburst," Michelle remarked with a tad more bitterness than she had intended. She really did want to try to keep things civil and not treat him like she was a scorned lover.

"Yeah, about that. I'm sorry if I overreacted a bit. I was just feeling really guilty, and things aren't going well at home. Lucy and I are fighting even more now than ever. She actually accused me of cheating on her. Can you believe that? I've never cheated on her. Ever. Well, at least not until you came into my life. Now all I can think about is you. Your smile, your laugh, the way you look at me."

The way I look at him?

Michelle started wondering if she was right, that she had been giving her feelings away before she was even consciously aware of them. *Damnit*, she thought.

"Look, Mike. I am really sorry if I have been looking at you in a way that isn't appropriate. I do really care for you. I don't have many friends here, and we've become really close. I really enjoy spending time with you, whether we are working together or just talking. I'm unsure how we got here, and a part of me is really scared because I have never felt this connected to anyone. No one has ever taken the time to get to know me like you have, and oddly,

I feel safe sharing my deep, dark secrets with you. As much as I kept telling myself to keep a professional distance because you're my boss, the long hours we work make it really hard. I'm really sorry if I let things go too far. I'm having a hard time reining in how I feel, if I am being honest. It feels like we have chemistry because even when you touch my arm, I feel the electricity from head to toe! It's really hard to ignore and pretend it isn't there. And please, please tell me to quit talking because I'm babbling and saying way too much. You have this effect on me where I want to share everything running through my head because you make me feel so safe." (Notice she is taking full accountability for something he initiated!)

Mike ran his fingers through his hair and exhaled deeply, a gesture she now found endearing. She'd noticed that it was something he did when he was feeling overwhelmed and needed a minute to gather his thoughts.

"Wow! I wasn't expecting all of that." He paused, then continued, "But, of course, I feel the chemistry. It is hard to deny; it's why I didn't pull away when you kissed me. But then Lucy texted me, and I was pulled back into reality. The crushing guilt I felt consumed me. I don't know what to say. I feel so honored that a girl like you could fall for a guy like me. You're way out of my league in so many ways, and there are things I'd love to do with you that I can't mention here. If we had met fifteen years ago, things would be so different. But right now, we have to figure out how to handle this." (Notice how he subtly shifted the blame to her for the kiss that *he* initiated.)

Handle this? What does that mean? Is he worried about losing his job? Or does he mean handle it from an HR perspective? Or does he mean our relationship, if that even is what this is? Does he mean his wife?

Unsure, Michelle responded by putting the ball back in his court. Two can play this game, and she wanted to know exactly what he meant. "Okay. How do you think we should move forward?" she asked.

"I've spent a lot of time contemplating this. Obviously, neither one of us wants to get fired, nor do I want my wife to find out about us."

Us?

"I need to know I can trust you," Mike continues. "I need to know that you will keep this between us. You can't tell anyone about us. Trust is the most important thing if we are going to continue to be in each other's lives. I can't lose my family this way. It would be too devastating to my kids. I don't want them to think I am a total asshole. Lucy will poison them against me like my mother did to my dad. I don't want to lose them. I can't." (More grooming and manipulation by playing on her empathy. He was also using triangulation and manipulating her to gain control. He was subtly letting her know that he had more to lose than she did, so she would empathize and excuse away his behavior.)

"Of course. Of course! I would never want you to break up your family or cause you to lose your kids. I would feel terrible if that happened. I don't want to be responsible for that. Of course you can trust me. I won't say a word to anyone. I wouldn't want anyone to know I was involved with a married man anyway. It would make me look like a terrible person," Michelle quickly replied. (Mike now had her exactly where he wanted her. She was taking responsibility for nearly everything, and because of her empathy, she would minimize her own needs and de-prioritize herself.)

Mike continued, "Okay, good. I am glad we are on the same page. This is so out of character for both of us. It would be terrible if anyone found out. It would be humiliating." (Here, he was sealing the deal with more manipulation by trying to remind her of how similar they were and that they had the same values so that she continued to trust him and by reinforcing all the reasons why she needed to keep quiet. His manipulation was serving him perfectly and allowing him to control her actions or inactions.)

Michelle nodded her head in agreement. "So now what? What should I do? Quit?" (She was acknowledging that he held the power in the relationship, whether it was conscious or subconscious, because she was looking to him to guide her, which was exactly where he wanted her, eating out of his palm. Notice how she automatically assumed that she would have to "fix things.")

"No, no. I want us to keep working together if that is okay with you. I don't want to stir things up. People might question it since we have been working so closely together. My advice would be to start figuring out what your next step might be, perhaps an internal transfer?" Mike said, trying to be helpful. (His advice let her clearly know that he was not going to help her and that it was her problem, not his. He was manipulating his position of power, undermining her sense of safety, and isolating her to figure things out alone, while protecting his self-image. If she were to quit, it would reflect poorly on him.)

Michelle's jaw fell nearly to the floor. On one hand, she was relieved she wasn't going to have to quit right away. On the other hand, she couldn't believe she would have to be the one to take the fall and initiate an internal transfer. Why wasn't he willing to explore options within the firm? Weren't they both in this together?

Mike perceived she was upset and quickly followed up with, "Michelle, I have a wife and kids and a mortgage to support. I need this job more than you do. You understand, don't you?" (Here he was using his self-importance to undermine hers by using what seems like a sound argument, but at the same time, it was whittling away at her own self-worth because she would agree and reinforce an underlying belief that she was not worthy of keeping her position and he was more worthy of keeping his job due to his responsibilities.)

Michelle blinked.

"Yes... yes, of course," she slowly replied. It made sense. Of course, it made sense when he put it that way. (She was rationalizing the lack of support.) He wasn't trying to threaten her. (Only control her to save himself!) He had a family, a mortgage, and private school tuition to pay. It wasn't unreasonable for him to assume she'd have to be the one to find another position. She saw that now. She understood the differences in their circumstances, and she felt bad that she put him in this position.

"I'm so sorry, Mike. I would never want you to risk your family's future. It's all my fault. I'm really, really sorry. I should've known better." (She was taking the fall without realizing that he manipulated her into apologizing and believing it was her fault and that now it was her job to fix it.)

She started to get up from her seat and he put his hand on her wrist.

"There's one more thing," Mike said. "I can count on you to be discreet, right? I wouldn't want your reputation to get tarnished—especially since you're up for a promotion. Why don't you reach out to HR and tell them you aren't sure the role is a good fit and ask to be transferred to another department within the firm?"

"Yeah, that's a good idea. I'll think about what to say and make the call later today," Michelle said quietly.

With that, she turned and left the café feeling as though her head was spinning and unsure of what had actually happened. She went there earlier believing she was going to get an apology. She left feeling almost depressed, guilty, and scared about how she had nearly broken up a family *and* lost her job, simultaneously. She was beginning to fear that she was becoming someone she didn't recognize, and she wasn't sure she liked it.

Michelle liked to play by the rules. She liked playing it safe. She hadn't rebelled since her senior of high school when she "borrowed" her mom's car one night to go to a party she was forbidden to attend, leaving her mom with no way of tracking her down (teenagers didn't have cell phones back then!).

As Michelle stepped off the elevator back onto her floor and made her way to her desk, she felt like she was in a trance. She couldn't believe she had agreed to call HR and ask for a transfer. Of course, she could see no other way. She hopped onto the firm's website and searched for internal opportunities in other areas of the firm. She noted a couple that seemed promising and interesting and made the phone call.

Mike didn't return to the office that afternoon, which was a relief. Michelle wasn't sure she could face him again after their talk. She felt so ashamed of herself. She also still felt thoroughly confused. She had no clue where she and Mike stood. Were they still going to be friends? Or were they just going to ignore each other until she got transferred to another department?

She decided she needed to make more friends in the city and that there was no better moment than the present. She turned around and asked Linda what she was doing after work and if she wanted to grab a drink. Lord knows Michelle could use a drink after everything that had transpired that morning. Linda was always up for a drink after work, so she quickly said yes. Kevin chimed in and asked if he could join.

"The more the merrier," Michelle responded a little too chirpily.

Reflections

In this chapter, Mike gaslit Michelle by making her believe she was the one who initiated the kiss. He then employed DARVO (deny, attack, reverse victim and offender) by attacking her and driving the point home that she was the one to blame (the offender) and that he was the victim.

Mike then gave Michelle the silent treatment after he confronted and blamed her for the kiss. He possibly felt guilty but couldn't accept the guilt, so he used the silent treatment as a way to wear her down mentally and emotionally. He then took advantage of her weakened state to get her to accept that she was the one who was at fault and that all the responsibility was hers.

We also witnessed an isolation tactic, when Mike subtly iced Michelle out and told her that she needed to figure out her next step and find another position in the firm to avoid having their relationship discovered. He didn't provide any emotional support. He isolated her by putting the responsibility and accountability on her shoulders, leaving her alone to figure out the solution to a mutual problem.

Chapter Six

HOOVER—WAIT, COME BACK!

That night at the bar, Michelle drank a little too much. She, Linda, and Kevin stayed through happy hour and then decided to forgo dinner and do shots instead. It was a summer Friday, after all. Turns out, however, that it was a bad idea. A really bad idea. Michelle's head began to spin.

She began fussing for her phone and wrestled it out of her impossibly small bag to check the time, just as it started to vibrate.

It was a text from Mike.

Her heart stopped. She quickly excused herself and practically ran toward the ladies' room.

Kevin and Linda looked at each other and laughed. "Well, someone has had too much to drink!" they yelled after her.

Michelle ignored them and kept going. Once she was safely inside the stall, she unlocked her phone and read Mike's message.

"Hey, I just want you to know how much I appreciate you and how much I care about you. This isn't easy for me. I have no idea what's going to happen over here, but I do know that I don't want to give Lucy any ammunition to keep my kids away from me if things blow up. I don't want to lose your friendship and whatever potential there is between us, because it's unique and special." (Trying to keep access to his narcissistic supply.)

Michelle had to read it three more times to make sense of it. She knew she had drunk a little too much but for some reason, her mind was really struggling with how she was meant to respond and how she felt about what she had just read. Was she supposed to respond? Was she supposed to agree to remaining friends? Was she supposed to remain open to possibilities? Or was he asking her to stay away? It was all so confusing!

Just as she was about to start typing some semblance of a response, Linda came barging into the bathroom slurring, "Hey Miiiichellllllle! Are you still in 'ere? You okay?"

Michelle flushed the toilet, pretending she was just finishing up, and exited the stall. As she washed her hands, Linda watched her quizzically.

"Are you okayyyy? You don't seeeeeem okayyy?" she slurred.

"I'm okay, I think I might have overdone it. I need to go home. Home sweet home. Tell Kevin I said goodbye. See you Monday! And Linda, thanks for having a drink with me!" Michelle responded.

"Or seven," Linda trilled. "Seeeeee you Mondaaay."

* * *

Michelle decided to walk home, hoping the crisp, cool evening air would help clear her head. As she was about to cross the street, she nearly twisted her ankle stepping on a cobblestone, one of the many charms of downtown Manhattan. A man quickly rushed to her side and steadied her by the elbow.

"Careful there!" he said.

Michelle turned toward the man. She recognized his voice but also the familiar sense of electricity shooting up and down her arm from where he had touched her.

"Mike?" she said, and she crumpled into a heap of tears on the street corner.

Mike quickly scanned the perimeter to see if anyone was watching them. Then he bent down and asked, "Are you okay?" This was quickly followed by, "Have you been drinking?"

Michelle could barely compose herself between sobs. There was a small part of her that was wondering if she was imagining him. Finally, she took a few deep breaths, wiped her eyes with the back of her hands, and found the strength to stand up and smooth out her dress.

She looked at him. Really looked at him. Well, as much as she could focus on him. After all, she was still drunk. While slightly swaying, she flatly answered, "Yes, I have been drinking. After work, I went out with Kevin and…"

Before she could finish her sentence, he grabbed her by the shoulders, looked her straight in the eye, and said, "You were out with Kevin? I tell you how much you mean to me and how much I value our relationship and just because I can't exactly storm out on my wife and kids, you decide to go out with Kevin?!"

Mike released Michelle from his grip, exhaled audibly, started pacing, and ran his fingers through his hair, while mumbling, "Unbelievable. I can't believe it. I'm an idiot! A true, bona fide idiot! I was willing to leave my wife for you and you go and replace me with Kevin the first chance you get?!" His voice was growing louder and louder with each word. (A display of extreme jealousy.)

Huh? Replace? What? Michelle couldn't follow his stream of consciousness but was about to explain when he stormed back over to her and said through gritted teeth, "I can tell this is all a game to you, isn't it? You don't really care. Hell, you probably thought that I would be your fast track to a promotion, huh? You don't care about me. If you did, you wouldn't have turned around and went out on a date with Kevin after I told you that I had feelings for you!"

Had he told her earlier today that he had feelings for her? She wasn't quite sure. Michelle also couldn't discern if she should be scared of his irrational reaction or angry at his accusations. She decided it was the latter.

"Are you serious right now? Kevin? You think I would go out with Kevin? I was actually out with Kevin *and* Linda, if you really want to know. But even if I did go out with Kevin, what would be so wrong with that? At least he's not my boss *and* he's *not* married! It would be perfectly reasonable for a single woman like me to go out with a single man like Kevin, *IF* I wanted to and *IF* I was interested," Michelle shouted back.

"So, is that what you want? You want a single guy like Kevin who wouldn't know how to treat a woman even if she came with an instruction manual!? He sure as hell would never appreciate a woman like you. You're too sophisticated for him, too smart, and way out of his league!" Mike retorted. (He's slowly hoovering her back in through manipulation.)

"Unlike you, Mike? Because *you* know how to treat a woman? Is that so?" Michelle said with her hands on her hips.

"I sure as hell know a lot more than that bozo. And if we weren't standing in the middle of a street corner, I'd take you in my arms and show you exactly how you deserve to be treated."

Michelle's mouth fell wide open. She was sure it nearly hit the curb because here he was, saying things again that made her stomach do funny things and her head go fuzzy (or maybe that was from the alcohol?).

Mike took two swift steps toward her and asked her if she'd like to go somewhere a bit more private to talk. Michelle hesitated before slowly shaking her head. Quietly she said she had to go home. Having this conversation after a few drinks was not a good idea. She didn't trust herself and she wasn't sure she trusted Mike either, for some reason. (She was starting to possibly notice some red flags and her intuition was likely letting her know he couldn't be trusted because his words and actions didn't jibe.)

It felt like every conversation she had with him led her to becoming more and more confused. Was it the alcohol clouding her mind or was her memory just really bad from the lack of sleep and stress? She sometimes felt that talking to Mike was like doing mental and emotional gymnastics. (Gaslighting and manipulation.) She couldn't keep their conversations straight, and emotionally, he seemed to be all over the place, which made her own emotions even harder to understand.

Mike apologized for being too forward. "I really do just want to talk. I would never pressure you into something that made you feel uncomfortable. I realize I am a little bit all over the place, but I'm so torn between doing what I want to do and doing what I know is right. You understand, right? It kind of feels like I'm a kid in a candy store—I want all of it—but I'm diabetic." (Trying to throw her off by disarming her and trying to show her he's a good guy.)

"Wait, what? Did you just compare yourself to a diabetic kid? And are you insinuating that I am the candy?" Michelle started laughing and then couldn't stop. Yes, the alcohol had something to do with why she found it so incredibly funny.

Mike looked away, as if he was hurt or maybe angry that she was laughing at him.

Michelle noticed and tried, between snorts, to quickly compose herself. She put her hand on his shoulder. "I'm sorry, Mike. I'm not laughing at you. It was just a really funny and kind of random analogy. I didn't mean to hurt your feelings." (She was always quick to apologize and was hypervigilant to his feelings.)

"It's okay, but truthfully, it feels a bit like you are mocking me. I was just trying to explain that I would never do anything to make you uncomfortable but was hoping you'd understand how hard this all is for me. I feel like you're making me out to be a bad guy, when all I've been is a good guy. I've listened to you and offered you advice to help you with your relationship with your mother, I've taken you under my wing at work, and I've been a good friend to you. Meanwhile, you're the one who is constantly apologizing for something you did and now you're laughing at me. A guy can only take so much." (Here he was gaslighting and manipulating her by playing the victim and making her out to be the perpetrator [DARVO].)

"You're right. I am so sorry, Mike. Honestly, I didn't mean to make you feel bad. I really do value our relationship, whatever it is that we are. You are a stand-up guy, and I know you're in a tough spot with your wife right now. Maybe we should stop talking for a bit, outside of work, that is. We could probably both use some space." (She was taking blame for some things she didn't do. Technically, she hasn't done anything wrong, as he has initiated the entire relationship and blamed it all on her. She was also buying into his story that he's the good guy and the victim, which subconsciously makes her the bad guy.)

Mike was quiet for a minute, looked away, and then back at her. "I don't want space. I don't need time apart. My marriage is on life support, if it hasn't already flatlined, and I know that I want to keep talking to you. You are the one person who makes me feel alive. As for everything else, I don't know what to do." (He was hoovering her back in, while still playing the victim.)

Michelle responded, "Okay, well, I will leave the ball in your court. If you need some space to figure things out, I completely understand. I want you to know I won't be offended. I'm glad you don't want to stop talking because to be honest, that week when you gave me the silent treatment was the worst week I've had in a long, long time!"

Mike smiled mischievously. "Well, don't ever give me a reason again to give you the silent treatment and it won't be an issue!"

Nervous laughter erupted from somewhere deep inside Michelle. She wasn't sure if that was a veiled threat or a joke. She decided to let it go. Her head was starting to spin again, and a headache was about to ensue. She was not sure how to end this conversation, but she knew it was best for them each to go home before Linda and Kevin left the bar down the street and spotted them.

"I better get home before my phone starts blowing up. Are you okay getting home alone?"

Michelle nodded.

"Okay, well... goodnight, Michelle. I'll reach out over the weekend when I can. If I don't for some reason, know I'll be thinking about you and can't wait to see your smiling face bright and early on Monday morning." He leaned down and kissed her on the cheek.

"G'night. See you on Monday," Michelle responded rather breathlessly.

Mike winked at her as he hailed a cab, hopped in, and it sped away.

A minute later, another cab pulled up and Michelle rode home thinking about how she was not sure why but there was a part of her that felt a little unsettled. She brushed it aside, chalking it up to the dulling effect of the alcohol and closed her eyes until the cab pulled up in front of her apartment building. She hoped to hear from Mike over the weekend, but she had learned not to get her hopes up. (She was settling for breadcrumbs, likely because she was used to accepting less than she deserves.)

As the weekend went on, Michelle had a lot of downtime to really think everything through. She was still not sure where she stood with Mike. The call with HR, however, went well on Friday.

All her accolades from working with Mike should help her easily find another role within the firm. She felt good about that, even if she was sad that she'd no longer be working with Mike, Kevin, and Linda.

Michelle just could not seem to find any kind of clarity around everything with Mike. Should they even be friends? Could she handle just being friends? Could he handle just being friends, or would he constantly feel guilty and pull away, to only then profess how he felt? (She may have begun to recognize the pattern of love and rejection followed by hoovering.)

She came to the conclusion that, for now, she should focus on getting a transfer and keep things professional with Mike. When and *if* he and Lucy separated, then perhaps they could be friends and talk more regularly about their personal lives. For now, she decided she needed some space.

The mere idea of taking space felt foreign to Michelle. She wasn't used to being the one to ask for space. If she was honest, she was usually the kind of girl who loved to spend as much time as possible with the guy she was dating, pulling back from all of her own interests, and sometimes even forgoing her friends. She was not sure why she had drawn this conclusion of needing space, but for some reason, it felt like maybe it might be best—not just for her but also for Mike so he could figure out what he wanted. (As a codependent, she'd be more willing to take space if she thought it was what was best for Mike, ignoring what she needed for herself to sort things out and enforce boundaries.)

Michelle was determined not to lose herself in a relationship again, even if that relationship was just a friendship right now. *Ugh, how did I get here?* she silently scolded herself. *When did everything become so complicated? And confusing? And if I feel this way, then Mike must feel this in amplification because his situation is much more tenuous and could impact more than just him.* (Michelle minimized her own feelings and predicament.)

Michelle pulled the covers over her head and decided to go to bed early to stop this torturous line of thinking. She didn't hear from Mike all weekend, and while she was disappointed, she wasn't surprised. She knew he was probably busy with his kids.

The following morning as Michelle stood before her reflection in the mirror, she practiced the speech she planned on giving Mike later that day. She was nervous, but she knew in her heart that it was what Mike needed to hear to take the pressure off him.

Hours later, she finally corralled Mike into the conference room to discuss some confidential details of the project they were working on.

"Hey, so what's going on? Fill me in," Mike asks, still believing Michelle wanted to talk about work.

"Oh, sorry! I don't really have confidential details to discuss. I just wanted to speak with you in private for a minute. Is that okay?"

"Of course, but let's make it quick so people aren't wondering what we are doing in here," he said with a slick grin.

"Haha! I really hope people don't start gossiping; that would be awful!" Michelle said with some concern. "Listen," she continued, "I'll keep this brief, but I've had a lot of time to think about things this weekend. As you probably presume already, I called HR on Friday, and they are working on finding me another opportunity within the firm. In the meantime, I think it might be best for you, given everything that's going on, if we take some space."

Michelle could see the wheels turning in Mike's head as he was contemplating what she was saying so he could thoughtfully respond. "Space. You think space is something I need right now?"

"Well, yes," Michelle fumbled. "Maybe? Don't you agree? I think it might be best right now, given everything, so you can clear your head and figure out what you want."

"I know what I want," Mike said playfully, tugging at her hip so she had to move in closer. He bit his lip.

Michelle felt uncomfortable, knowing her colleagues were right outside the door, yet also confused.

"Okay, but what about Lucy? Your kids? Your life? Your whole life *outside* of this office?" Michelle asked earnestly but also with frustration. "Are you willing to just throw that all out the window all of a sudden for a hot young thang in the office?"

Michelle realized she said all of that with a bit more anger and sass than she had intended to, but it was true. Mike had this way of making her feel safe, understood, and cared for, yet at the same time, he also had such an abrasive way of cutting her down.

Mike immediately threw his hands up. "Whoa! I am feeling slightly like I am being attacked. Are you giving me an ultimatum?"

"Wait, what?" Michelle asked incredulously. She couldn't believe that he thought she was giving him an ultimatum. Yes, she had gotten a little frustrated but offered to give him space to make things easier on him, not put more pressure on him. How did he not see that?

"I'm only trying to help make things easier, not harder, by removing myself from this complicated situation," Michelle responded.

"So, basically, you are saying that *you* want space, but you are pretending like it's for my own good rather than stating that it's what *you* want? Is that what you want? Space from me?" Mike asked.

"Huh? No! I don't want space from you. I just thought it might help you because you seem confused, that's all." Michelle replied nervously. A part of her was afraid he would say yes and walk out of the room. Another part of her feared what would happen if they *didn't* take time apart. What if they continued to grow closer and closer? Would it become harder and harder to remain friends when their chemistry felt so undeniable? Michelle started to pace, trying to ground herself. She wasn't sure if she wanted to fight to not take space or flee the room and take the space she thought he needed.

Mike clenched his jaw and said through gritted teeth, clearly annoyed, "You think you know what's best for me? Do you think I can't handle figuring out what I need? Do I seem incapable to you? If I need space, I will ask for it. I think you are the one who needs space, and maybe I was wrong about how you feel about me. Maybe this is just a game to you, but it's not to me, Michelle." (He was trying to keep control and make her question herself by projecting. This was a covert way of gaslighting her by turning things around so that she ultimately mistrusted her own judgment and what she felt was best, even if it was under the guise of doing it for his good. It was also his way of getting his supply by subtly inciting her to flood him with reassurances of how much she cared. As a codependent, it is easier to do something hard when you believe you are doing it for the best interest of those you care about, never for your own needs/wants/desires. He was preying on this dynamic by projecting and twisting it around on her.)

Michelle froze. She wasn't sure how to respond, but she was shocked that he had actually just accused her of playing games! She also didn't like that she was being attacked for trying to do what she thought might be best for Mike. He made it clear he didn't want or need her help. Maybe she needed to trust that *he* knew what was best for him. For some reason, everything he just said left her feeling wildly unsettled, and she couldn't make sense of all the emotions she was feeling: shame, rejection, empathy, and insulted all at once.

Michelle was in a tailspin. Hadn't she meant to let Mike know that she empathized with his situation and that if he needed space, she would completely understand? How was he turning it around on her? How could he think she didn't care about him and that this was all a game to her? Anger. That was the emotion she landed on after trying to process all the other emotions that had bubbled up. The anger felt safer.

"A game? You think this is a *game* to me? I was merely trying to help *you* because I understand how difficult this must be for you. You know I care about you. I care about you a whole lot. Maybe you're right. Maybe I do need some space, Mike. Clearly, this relationship is creating too much chaos for both of us." With that, Michelle turned to leave.

Mike quickly grabbed her wrist, put his head down, and softly apologized for insinuating that this was a game to her. (Hoovering her back in.) She looked at him, but he noticed a fierceness in her eyes. He was slowly losing her. So, he began overexplaining why he was so on edge and how he hadn't meant to hurt her. That it was only because he and Lucy had been fighting yet again this morning, and so he'd been angry and on the defensive ever since. He apologized for taking it out on her.

Michelle softened a little. She accepted his apology and told him she understood, just to keep the peace, and walked out.

Michelle kept walking until she got to the stairwell. She decided walking down twelve flights of stairs would be good for her because she needed to burn off her anger and frustration.

Halfway down the stairs, as she reflected on their relatively short past, she recognized a pattern emerging in Mike's behavior. She recognized that more recently, when she was around Mike, she tended to walk away feeling more conflicted than happy. She could see how after each altercation, she felt like she was lost in a fog of confusion more often than not. She wasn't sure why she found interactions with him disorienting, and she wondered what happened to the early days when they would just talk and share stories, laugh, and enjoy each other's company. They were both always apologizing for something. Maybe they were hurting each other more than helping each other. Either way, she came to the conclusion that it wasn't healthy and that it was time to make sure she got the transfer through HR.

Reflections

Thus far in the story, Mike has used the tactic of triangulation in several variations. Clearly, there was already a triangle because Mike was a married man, but he used this to his advantage to manipulate and control Michelle. Mike tried to triangulate Michelle initially with his wife by claiming himself to be the victim of a bad marriage, Lucy as the villain, and Michelle as the understanding, empathetic support he needed and didn't have elsewhere. He referenced how Michelle understood Mike better than Lucy, yet later he cast Michelle as the villain and himself as the victim with his family as the most important priority, leaving Michelle feeling unimportant and at the same time, *responsible* for putting Mike in a situation where he had to choose between her and his family. This was a situation he manipulated her into in the first place. He later also tried to implicate Kevin into his triangulation tactics by feigning jealousy to incite Michelle to proffer reassurances.

In this last cycle of abuse, we saw Mike employing so many narcissistic tactics as he was desperate to get what he wanted: to keep his position of power and control and his narcissistic supply, all without risking anything in order to maintain them, but rather, manipulating Michelle into sacrificing her needs, wants, dreams, and desires. He used love bombing, gaslighting, subtle and more overt DARVO tactics, isolation, and triangulation tactics. He was pulling from his bag of tricks to keep her in some semblance of a relationship that served his needs while not damaging his self-image or position.

Chapter Seven

CONCLUSION AND REFLECTION— EMPOWERED GOODBYE

Michelle finally got the transfer to another department within the firm. As she packed up her desk on her last day working for Mike, he brought her an orchid to wish her well. It was unexpected, and she coughed, choking on the lump in her throat as she fought back tears.

The last couple of weeks had been hard seeing him every day. She knew what she was doing was for the best for both of them. She no longer wanted to be caught between Mike and his wife, not even as a friend. She had ignored his calls and tried to avoid him at work as best she could. When no one was looking, he had tried slipping her notes, which she carefully put in her pocket and then ran through the shredding machine in the copy room. He sent her text messages telling her how much he missed her and how sorry he was. It took every ounce of her willpower not to respond.

A part of her grieved the potential of the relationship. Another part of her grieved the loss of the job she enjoyed, even though she was excited to start working in another area of the firm. She also grieved for Mike and Lucy because she felt partly responsible for their issues, even if they started long before she met Mike.

Michelle knew she'd have to be careful not to let Mike back into her life or her heart because he had already left a gaping hole that she was trying to fill with distractions. She had taken up painting and dance cardio classes to cope.

And then, just as she was about to thank Mike for the orchid and carry her box of belongings to her new desk on the eighteenth floor, she caught him smirking at the new intern who worked not ten feet away from where she was standing. It was the same smirk he used to give her when no one was looking. At that moment, Michelle wanted to chuck the orchid at his head, pot and all, but she held her head high and silently wished Mike's innocent new target good luck, thankful that she got out before she got in too deep. *Crisis narrowly averted,* she thought.

Reflections

Upon reading Mike and Michelle's story, did you find any parallels between what Michelle experienced and your own life or someone close to you?

Mike manipulated Michelle by playing on her empathy and her desire to be helpful, supportive, and a good friend with the added entanglement that they were also colleagues where there was already an imbalance of power. We can see her codependent tendencies shining through, which kept her unaware of how her patterns of behavior embroiled her into this toxic dynamic by not having clear and strong boundaries and by over-caring.

We're going to spend the next several chapters digging deeper into why we attract these types of personalities and why it can be hard to break free. We'll then explore how to begin healing from the trauma of narcissistic abuse.

Part Three

Deep Dive into Narcissistic Trauma, Dysfunctional Family Dynamics, and the Wounds They Leave Behind

Chapter Eight

HOW DO WE END UP IN THESE TOXIC RELATIONSHIPS?

We end up in these narcissistic relationships because the patterns that are present are often familiar from childhood. The foundation is in codependency, which has become normalized in our society. The movies we watch, the media we consume, the music we listen to are all riddled with codependency. I can't help but think about that scene in *Jerry Maguire* when Tom Cruise says to Renée Zellweger, "You complete me." How many of us swooned at that line and harbored a deep desire to have a partner who would say something like that to us? It seemed so romantic, right?

Except that it's really *not* healthy. It's *not* healthy to expect another person to fill us up and to provide the missing pieces. In order to create a healthy interdependent relationship, we need to come *from* a place of wholeness. When we enter into a relationship from a place of wholeness, we avoid overcompensating for a lack of self-love because we have it within ourselves. When we know our value and our worth, and we are able to self-accept, there's no need to find validations or approval from others.

We stop settling for unhealthy love when we cultivate a *healthy* sense of self-love. The way we do that is by first knowing who we are on a deep level. Just like you couldn't fall in love with someone you didn't know, you need to know yourself intimately in order to fully and deeply love and accept yourself as well.

The tool I have found that has been profoundly impactful on me and my clients is Human Design, a beautiful self-discovery tool that blends together ancient and modern wisdoms, creating a unique blueprint of the potential of who you are. It doesn't label you or put you in a box. You get to decide how you want to embody the various aspects of your Human Design chart and how you want to bring it to life. You get to choose how you express the beauty and story of who you are in a way that brings you joy and that allows you to use the natural talents and gifts that come easily to you.

The chart can show you where you may be stuck or living out a lower expression of what's possible. It can indicate where you may have a propensity toward leaning into codependency either via victimhood or martyrdom. It can show you where you may be compromising your value, values, or authenticity for the sake of others. It can show you where maybe you're sharing insights, opinions, or inspiration before people are ready, causing you to feel unseen, unheard, or misunderstood. It can also show where you may potentially be holding on to a toxic relationship (or anything) for longer than you should.

Your Human Design blueprint is not a diagnostic tool but rather it provides a road map to understanding how you can begin living your life in greater alignment with your soul and life purpose. It can show you the role you are here to play, how you're meant to make big decisions, and how you're meant to use your energy in the world, so you don't burn out.

Once you are able to see yourself through this different perspective, you'll be able to slowly begin accepting all of who you are. Once you can accept yourself fully for being *you*, you can begin to learn how to love yourself. Once you love and accept yourself fully and completely, you will be able to trust and know that you are worthy of love, happiness, and a deeply meaningful relationship just simply because you exist.

This is what I want for every single one of you reading this book right now:
- To love yourself so completely that you no longer settle for being treated in a way that is so much less than you deserve

- To know you are worthy of love without strings attached, without having to do anything or be someone you're not
- To be able to set and maintain boundaries as an act of self-love so you always feel safe being authentically you
- To feel safe enough to be vulnerable, keeping your heart wide open as you connect with others and the world around you
- To trust yourself enough to know you are capable of making good, healthy choices
- To know the abuse you suffered wasn't your fault and that you deserve *so* much better
- To know that a brighter, more peaceful life is waiting for you—one filled with the love and joy you've always deserved

Part of the reason you may have ended up in these toxic relationships is likely because you are codependent. Now, you may be reading this thinking, *I am hyper-independent! How can I possibly be codependent!?* Well, the two are not mutually exclusive, and I'll dive deeper into why after we first discuss what codependency is.

What Is a Codependent and Why Do They Magnetize Narcissists?

When the word *codependent* was first coined, it described someone whose partner suffered from substance abuse. The codependent was the enabler who made excuses for their alcoholic or drug-addicted partner.

Since then, the word *codependent* has evolved to refer to someone who relies on someone else to support their value, worth, and sense of lovability. More succinctly, codependents rely on someone else to boost their self-esteem and validate them due to a deep underlying insecurity.

They often seek out or attract partners with similar patterns of behavior. These dynamics are typically rooted in their childhood experiences, where one or both parents may have also been codependent. As a result, when they encounter someone who feels "safe," it is often because the behavior aligns with the familiar patterns they grew up with. We tend to feel safe in what feels familiar.

Codependents typically fall into one of three roles in their relationships as depicted in psychiatrist Stephen B. Karpman's Drama Triangle that he introduced in 1968:

Karpman Drama Triangle

The Persecutor: In this role, the person does not value other people or their perspectives. They can appear angry (openly or passively), aggressive, judgmental, spiteful, or scornful. They may also bully others or be demanding. They may more readily blame others and act aggressively in order to exert control.

The Victim: In this role, the person does not value themselves and may defer to others. They can appear manipulative, helpless, needy, fretful, or downtrodden. They may have a poor-me mentality, or they may complain or whine often and blame others for why things always happen to them. They may feel repressed or stuck and expect others to rescue them from their dire circumstances.

The Rescuer: In this role, the person does not believe others are capable of helping themselves and is prone to martyrdom. They can appear self-sacrificing, over-helpful and facilitative, engulfing, or overbearing. They like to be needed and may be prone to meddling unnecessarily. They tend to step in and try to solve other people's problems without consent or being asked.

It's important to note that in codependent relationships, we unconsciously dance around the triangle, playing various roles within our relationships. Two people in a relationship will rarely play the same role at the same time, but rather take one of the opposing roles. Therefore, if one is playing the victim, the other may be playing the rescuer, for example. If perhaps, the victim isn't getting the attention, reassurance, or affection they need, they may become the persecutor, leading the other to then slip from the role of rescuer into the victim role.

Oftentimes, the persecutor is the role where we would find the narcissist in the drama triangle, but I assure you, the narcissist may also play the victim or the rescuer if it suits the outcome they seek. Therefore, we cannot define the persecutor as the narcissist.

The best way to exit this drama triangle is to, first, become aware of the patterns and, second, learn how to set clear, firm, and healthy boundaries in order to disrupt them. Exiting the triangle can be difficult if you are not used to setting boundaries or if you find the repercussions of setting them too difficult to navigate. This is where the work comes in to bolster your self-confidence and courage so you can effectively communicate, assert, and uphold the boundaries that are reflective of your worth and value. You may also need to work with your nervous system to overcome any uncomfortable or anxious feelings that may arise when you first begin setting boundaries.

As mentioned, codependents often gravitate toward partners who share similar codependent tendencies. Interestingly, while it may seem counterintuitive, all narcissists can also be considered codependents, though not all codependents are narcissists. Some are people pleasers and/or empaths. The defining traits that primarily delineate a narcissist from other codependents are little to no empathy, a lack of self-awareness, and a tendency to be self-centered; these traits are often accompanied by arrogance, though not always. Narcissists will also struggle to show true remorse and instead shift the blame to someone or something else.

See below for a breakdown of the similarities between a narcissist and other types of codependents.

Similarities:

NARCISSIST	(OTHER) CODEPENDENT
Codependent	Codependent
Deeply insecure	Deeply insecure
Learned/subconscious behavioral patterns	Learned/subconscious behavioral patterns
Manipulative (in a toxic way where they hurt others)	Manipulative (where they only hurt themselves)
Fear of not being lovable => fear of abandonment	Fear of rejection → fear of abandonment
Self-conscious	Self-conscious

Now, let's look at the differences that complement each other and strengthen the attraction between the two:

NARCISSIST	(OTHER) CODEPENDENT
Does not accept accountability or show remorse (never apologizes by admitting wrongdoing)	Often feels guilty and accepts blame (over-apologizes) readily
Disabler (disconnects others from power)	Enabler (makes excuses for others' bad behavior) due to a high degree of empathy
Seeks control to cope (coercive control)	Gives up control easily; self-abandons (although may still be independent)
Deep desire to be admired and adored and to feel superior	Deep desire to be accepted, liked, and to belong
Projects their own self-criticism onto others (overly critical of others)	Overly self-critical (does not project this on to others)

Fear of being seen for who they are (mask of overconfidence, superiority, grandiosity)	Fear of being seen for who they are (mask of being who they think others want them to be, existing to meet others' expectations)
Addictive personality (substances, sex, adoration, attention, porn, feeding their ego)	Addicted to love/oxytocin release (and recognition/attention)
Low empathy	Empaths/Empathetic
Avoids shame at all costs by shifting blame onto others to avoid feeling any pain	Shame drives guilt and acceptance of misplaced blame
Does not trust anyone; highly skeptical; may be paranoid	Trusts people easily; naive; may be more optimistic (sees the good in people)
Black-and-white (all-or-nothing, good-or-bad) thinking, called splitting	Black, white, and gray thinking (not all-or-nothing thinking)
People abuser (coping mechanisms are abusive)	People pleaser

    Now, these traits are not black and white. There are gray areas as well. Neither the narcissist nor the codependent will exhibit all of the qualities, behaviors, or traits above. They may exhibit some and not others and vary in degree.

    In some instances, codependents may mirror narcissistic behavior as a way to stay safe in the relationship. The difference will be whether they are able to express empathy, show remorse, and take accountability for their actions.

    As you can see by viewing the chart above, if you have more of an external focus on other people and identify as a people pleaser or someone who likes to make others happy by going out of your way, then you likely spend more time focusing on the needs of other people rather than your own.

This is the perfect match for a narcissist who is only concerned with themselves and getting their needs met.

If you are someone who has a hard time saying no or setting boundaries, then this will play very well into the unhealthy tactics of a narcissist, who will be able to easily manipulate you and keep the upper hand in the relationship.

If you tend to over-apologize or easily accept accountability even when it's not your fault just to keep the peace in your relationships, then this dynamic will work nicely with the narcissist who will never take accountability for their actions or show remorse.

If you tend to avoid speaking your truth as a way to avoid confrontation, then the narcissist will also appreciate this since you will likely back down easily in the face of conflict, which caters to their need for power and control. You may also not call them out on their toxic behavior if you fear it will lead to conflict or uncomfortable situations. Of course, this may be reinforced by their overly reactive behavior which escalates even during the most minor of offenses, conditioning you to "go along to get along."

If you are overly self-critical, then this too works well for the narcissist because they will likely project their own insecurities onto you, and you may easily accept them as your own, especially if you also identify as a people pleaser or have struggled with a strong understanding of who you are.

Can Someone Be Independent AND Codependent?

The answer is yes! While the two traits may seem contradictory, they can in fact coexist. A codependent may have learned early in life that relying on others wasn't safe. Perhaps they had a caregiver who was emotionally negligent, dismissive, or manipulative. Repeated experiences of feeling unsupported and disappointed by their caregivers taught them to rely solely on themselves. As a result, their independence, or even hyper-independence, developed as a coping mechanism.

That being said, a deep desire for approval, validation, or a sense of control over others remains beneath this independence.

An example of this would be someone who is highly independent and capable but who struggles to ask for help or feels guilty asking for support. They may also have a tendency to take on too much responsibility or feel accountable for the emotions or actions of others, both of which are common traits of a codependent.

It is important to recognize that codependent patterns and behaviors exist on a spectrum and may manifest differently. Someone who is exerting their independence in a coercive or abusive way to garner approval and validation would lean toward narcissistic characteristics, whereas someone who exerts their independence because they do not feel safe relying on others or because they feel responsible for everyone else would demonstrate more traditional codependent traits.

All in all, the impact of these behaviors distinguishes them further. A narcissist's behavior usually ends up hurting others, and they will deny any accountability and show no remorse. In contrast, a codependent's behavior usually ends up only hurting themselves, and if they unintentionally hurt someone else, they will be quick to apologize, take responsibility, and express guilt.

By understanding these nuances, we can better appreciate how independence and codependency can coexist while also recognizing their distinct motivations and outcomes.

Chapter Nine

Defining Trauma, Trauma Bonds, and the Four Trauma Responses

What Is Trauma?

According to dictionary.com, trauma is defined as:
1. Pathology.
   a. a body wound or shock produced by sudden physical injury, as from violence or accident.
   b. the condition produced by this; traumatism.
2. Psychiatry.
   a. an experience that produces psychological injury or pain.
   b. the psychological injury so caused.

When we consider narcissistic abuse, it's possible that there may be physical trauma if physical violence was a part of the relationship; however, once the bruises and scars heal, what is left behind are the invisible psychological and emotional wounds.

To further elucidate, trauma is anything that leaves an emotional charge that triggers a subconscious reaction as a result of something that happened in the past, whether the event was deemed traumatic or not. The trauma may be so deeply embedded in your subconscious that you may not be able to recall the events that created it in the first place.

Some of the lesser-known causes of trauma, for example, are moving homes or schools often as a child, being laughed at during a class presentation, being cursed at as a child by a caregiver, or experiencing parents getting divorced. That's just a few; there are plenty of other less obvious examples of trauma. This is why I prefer to use the definition of any event that may still hold an unresolved emotional charge.

The perceptions and meanings we give our past experiences are triggered in our relationships and in our day-to-day interactions.

For example, if you moved around a lot as a child, you may find it triggering to be in new social settings where you do not know anyone, especially if you were bullied and teased as a child for being the new kid. As a result, you may have developed coping strategies to overcome any feelings of discomfort in situations where you feel unsafe in a new environment. When you first meet someone new, you may find it difficult to trust them. Even gentle teasing can lead to an overreaction fueled by the fear of rejection, rooted in the trauma wounds you carry.

Sometimes, one of the coping strategies we adapt to avoid feeling the pain of those subconscious wounds is the suppression of emotions. This avoidance strategy is often used when triggered emotions feel too overwhelming or when we subconsciously perceive them as too unsafe to confront.

Another way we may mask the pain of our deep inner wounds is by numbing out through substance abuse, over-shopping, overeating, under-eating, social media scrolling, or binge-watching television.

Whenever we suppress our emotions, we create energy blockages in our bodies; after all, emotion is energy *in* motion. Over time, this stagnant energy can manifest physically as diseases or DIS-ease, such as autoimmune disorders, diabetes, high blood pressure, cancer, or chronic pain. Mentally, it can show up as anxiety, depression, or ADHD. Emotionally, it can lead to shutting down, dissociating, or becoming disconnected from our feelings altogether, including positive emotions like joy and love.

When we shut down our emotions, it's often because we don't feel safe expressing them or have been conditioned to believe they aren't safe to experience. Anger is a common example of an emotion we are often taught is not safe to feel or express. Yet, our emotions are actually here to teach us. They serve as messengers, offering us valuable lessons once we allow them to move through us. When suppressed, they have nowhere to go and can become stuck in the body, potentially leading to illnesses and ailments. What if we gave ourselves permission to actually feel our emotions and remained open and curious to uncover the wisdom they hold?

While our conscious mind knows that the trauma we have experienced is in the past, our bodies can continue to react as if the danger is still present. This is because our emotions are shaped by the perceptions and meanings we've attached to those past experiences. Emotions and thoughts are deeply interconnected, each influencing the other in a continuous feedback loop. When emotions remain unresolved, they become internalized as persistent feelings, subtly or overtly influencing how we speak, think, and interact with others. This is why true trauma healing must address both the mind and the body. As Bessel van der Kolk's book title on trauma states, *The Body Keeps the Score*. We'll dive deeper into this in chapter fifteen.

Four Trauma Responses

This physical storage of trauma often manifests through the body's instinctive responses to danger, also known as the four trauma responses: fight, flight, freeze, or fawn.

When we are triggered, a signal is sent from the hypothalamus in our brain to the autonomic nervous system, activating our sympathetic nervous system. As our nervous system moves from feeling safe, grounded, and connected (ventral vagal) into fight or flight (sympathetic), our autonomic nervous system sends a message to our adrenal glands, which sit on top of our kidneys to first release epinephrine (or adrenaline), which increases our heart rate, allowing the blood to flow away from our core to our limbs so we can either run toward the threat and fight it or run away from it to flee. Our breathing rate also quickens, and our airways open to take in more oxygen to stay alert in the presence of danger.

If we continue to perceive that we are in danger, whether consciously or subconsciously, then our adrenals will release cortisol to keep us hypervigilant and on edge so we can avoid any further threat. It is not until the perceived danger or threat passes that our cortisol levels drop and our parasympathetic (or ventral vagal state) nervous system kicks in, helping us feel calm again.

Without understanding anything further about the other two trauma or stress responses, you can see how if you have been in an ongoing abusive relationship, your body may constantly be pumping out cortisol to keep you safe. As a result, you may remain in a constantly reactive state, always on edge, walking on eggshells, or worrying about when the shoe will next drop. Elevated cortisol levels can cause inflammation in the body, leading to all kinds of health issues, diseases, and even cancer.

Sometimes when the body perceives the threat to be especially dangerous, the nervous system will move from the sympathetic (fight or flight) into a freeze or fawn response, which is a dorsal vagal state, a component of the parasympathetic nervous system. A fawn response is a please-and-appease response. It is what is more commonly known as people pleasing, whereby you may bypass your own needs entirely to attend to and serve the needs of others in order to stay safe. A fawn response has a similar biological effect as a freeze response. In both cases, you may have completely shut down or numbed your emotions, so you are not aware you have any needs or emotions of your own. When we spend lengthy periods of time in a freeze response, we dissociate from our bodies and disconnect from our emotions, even the good ones. In a freeze response, your heart rate slows down, as does your breathing, and you may experience things like depression, chronic fatigue, or prolonged exhaustion, or feel unable to enjoy the present moment.

Victims of narcissistic abuse may spend years vacillating between the sympathetic (fight or flight) and dorsal vagal (freeze or fawn) nervous system states, and it can be very hard to effectively downregulate your nervous system to feel safe again (ventral vagal state). However, I want you to know it absolutely is possible with the right support and tools! Let's dig deeper into the neurobiology so you can understand what is happening in your body when you get triggered.

What Is the Impact of Narcissistic Abuse on the Brain and Body?

If you have experienced ongoing narcissistic abuse, there is a likely chance that the amygdala, the part of your brain responsible for detecting danger, has become larger over time. This is how your body has adapted physiologically to chronic abuse.

Walking around on eggshells and waiting for the next big blowup can cause you to remain in a state of hypervigilance. As a result, your amygdala, which may have had to remain on high alert at all times to keep you safe, grows in size, while your prefrontal cortex, the part of the brain responsible for executive functioning, logical thinking, and decision-making, may shrink in size since it is being underutilized. As a result, you may struggle with brain fog and indecision. Finding the focus and motivation to get things done may also prove difficult because all of your energy is directed toward self-preservation.

Short-term memory issues may become apparent because the prefrontal cortex, which is also responsible for short-term memory recall, may have been impacted by the trauma you have experienced. The hippocampus, which stores your long-term memories, may suffer as well.

Once the amygdala signals danger, the hypothalamus, responsible for regulating the autonomic nervous system, stimulates the pituitary gland. The pituitary gland then secretes hormones that alert the adrenal glands to release adrenaline (epinephrine) followed by cortisol, preparing the body to respond to the perceived threat.

The hypothalamus-pituitary-adrenal connection is called the HPA axis. It is responsible for activating the fight or flight response in the body. The hormones it emits regulate many of the body's important functions, including respiration rate, heart rate, and digestion.

If you were being chased by a bear, the HPA axis would release hormones that would accelerate your breathing to increase the oxygen flow to your blood and raise your blood pressure to redirect blood flow away from your core to your outer extremities, enabling you to either fight or flee, all while triggering a state of hyperarousal. It also slows down digestion and weakens the immune system because your body needs all of its resources to fight off the impending danger.

Your prefrontal cortex also goes offline because you need to think not rationally or logically, but rather instinctually, in order to keep you safe. At this point, you are operating from your limbic system, the most primal part of the brain that relies on reactive, emotional, and instinctual responses to any threats or danger.

This is why, if you have experienced chronic abuse or trauma, you may suffer from brain fog as your cortex is offline and may, instead, be highly reactive (in your limbic brain). It can be difficult to make any clear decisions about whether to end the abusive relationship if you're stuck in a fight or flight response.

With this new understanding, I hope you are able to offer yourself some compassion and empathy as you navigate your next steps. You've been busy just trying to survive, and you may not have realized what you were experiencing is abuse. Or, if you did, it may have felt really difficult to figure out what to do next or to have the motivation, focus, or strength to follow through with your decision.

There are also other neurochemicals your brain releases throughout the abuse cycle that keep you stuck. It's part of what creates a trauma bond.

The vagus nerve (which is the internal superhighway that your autonomic nervous system operates along, known as the "wandering nerve") connects your brain to your gut. Along the way, it innervates the ears, throat, heart, lungs, and gut.

To help you overcome the overwhelm, I'd love to share with you a couple of somatic tools that I recommend to my clients.

Somatic tools help you work with your body's nervous system to promote emotional and psychological safety.

The first tool is called 2x breathing. This is not a technique I created; I first heard of it when I was learning how to meditate using Emily Fletcher's Ziva Technique, which I highly recommend.

You inhale for a count of two and then exhale for a count of four. After several rounds, increase your inhalation to a count of four and exhalation to a count of eight. The idea is that in extending the duration of your exhale for twice as long as your inhale, you are activating the parasympathetic nervous system to help you feel calm and at peace. If you were trying to outrun a bear, you wouldn't be able to exhale for twice as long as you inhale. Your breath would be shallower, so when you exhale for twice as long, you signal to your body you are safe. You are also stimulating the vagus nerve as you slow down your respiration rate.

I personally have used this technique countless times. The first time I became utterly convinced that it worked was when I started having an anxiety attack on an airplane during a very bumpy flight. I hope you will give it try; I promise you it works.

Another tool is to drink really cold water. Remember, when you are in fight or flight, all of the blood flow moves away from your core to your extremities so you can either defend yourself or run. By drinking really cold water, you bring back your attention to your core, a.k.a. your body, as you feel the cold water go down your esophagus to your stomach. Also, remember, the vagus nerve runs along your larynx all the way down to your gut, so you are stimulating it when you drink really cold water.

You could also activate the diver reflex by splashing cold water on your face and holding your breath. Again, you wouldn't be able to hold your breath if you had to outrun a predator; this signals to the parasympathetic branch of the vagus nerve that you are safe.

There are so many other somatic tools you could use. Having a toolkit of options and practicing them, even when you aren't in a state of stress or overwhelm, can help to increase the flexibility in your nervous system, which is important after years of experiencing chronic abuse and trauma. Use the QR code below to access a free guide to my top somatic tools to help you recover from narcissistic abuse.

If you have no idea how to scan a QR code, no worries! Just head to https://bit.ly/somatictoolsafternarcabuse.

What Is a Trauma Bond and What Is Its Effect on the Brain?

The cycle of abuse can have damaging effects on your brain chemistry because there are chemicals released throughout the cycle that your brain gets addicted to. This is why it's so hard to break a trauma bond.

A trauma bond forms when you form a deep attachment for someone who is abusing you, often accompanied by feelings of sympathy for them or a belief you cannot live without them. Oftentimes it is the chaos of the relationship that keeps you trapped in it.

As mentioned, the brain becomes addicted to the secretion of chemicals that are released during the high highs and the low lows. It's a combination of desperately seeking the love, validation, and approval during the highs and needing the lows to help you feel close again. Since the narcissist can appear to be a good person with bad qualities, you may feel they are not "that bad" and that overall "they are a good person," ignoring the impact and the toll the relationship is taking on you, your health, your self-worth, your sense of self, and your sense of lovability.

During the highs, your endocrine system secretes the happy love hormones: oxytocin, serotonin, and dopamine. During the lows, your adrenals secrete cortisol (a.k.a. the stress hormone), norepinephrine, and epinephrine. As a result, your body will crave the next high, trapping you in a pain/pleasure cycle and creating an addiction to the chaos. This happens because you become physically addicted to the neurochemicals released during the abuse cycle.

We often see that people in narcissistic relationships feel safe in the rollercoaster dynamic because it mirrors patterns from childhood. As a child, you may have had a parent who was overly critical, emotionally avoidant, or negligent, yet at times caring and affectionate. This alternating pattern of love mixed with rejection, criticism, or abuse can condition you to associate love with pain or struggle. Over time, you may have internalized the belief that love must be earned, that it is difficult, or that it inevitably hurts.

Once primed to accept this dysfunctional dynamic, you may have subconsciously sought out partners who replicate this familiar pattern by seeking the validation, approval, recognition, and love from your partner that you never received from your parent or caregiver. In essence, you may have been attempting to heal your childhood wounds through your adult relationships.

Besides the trauma bond and the fact that you may love them, the narcissist may also be manipulating you into believing that you can't survive without them, or that you won't be able to afford being on your own, or that no one else will put up with you or love you the way that they do. In a sense, the narcissist makes you dependent on them for validation, survival, love, or to meet your needs in some way (could be sexual, financial, or physical needs), and you easily allow that dynamic to play out because it is familiar from childhood.

Since the push/pull and chaos patterns of abuse, rejection, and love all seem normal to the non-narcissistic partner, he or she will confuse the abuse cycle with love. It reinforces their familiar version of love from childhood.

This brings up a very interesting dynamic. As mentioned, narcissists are also codependent. If codependents can change, does that mean a narcissist can change as well? We're going to explore this in the next chapter.

Chapter Ten

IS IT POSSIBLE FOR A NARCISSIST TO CHANGE?

Possible, yes. Likely, no. Anyone can change if they are willing to do the work and take accountability for their actions, but we know narcissists often struggle with this. They typically will shift the blame onto someone else or blame a situation or circumstance for their behavior.

So perhaps the better question is this: Are there any circumstances under which a narcissist is *willing* to change? Well, the answer is yes AND no.

First, we have to understand that a narcissist isn't born; they are created. Their behavior is learned in childhood as a way to cope with the deep pain they experienced, either from trauma or from having a parent or caregiver who was negligent, absent, substance dependent, or unable to meet their needs.

These maladaptive coping strategies developed subconsciously. The narcissist didn't intentionally or maliciously adopt these behaviors to hurt others. They did so rather subconsciously as a way to self-preserve because no one taught them any other healthy coping strategies. They may also have had a narcissistic parent who could not teach them empathy or how to respond in an emotionally appropriate way to the world around them. Remember, narcissists may have a low degree of empathy; they don't all necessarily lack it entirely.

As they mature and become adults, they may potentially become aware of the damage and impact their behavior has on others; however, the difference is that they will not take ownership or accountability for their actions. Instead, they blame the other person for why they reacted or behaved a certain way, or they blame a circumstance (i.e., really stressed out at work, didn't get enough sleep, etc.). They manipulate others into believing they (or some other circumstance) are to blame rather than taking responsibility for any wrongdoing. They will often use gaslighting as a tactic to deflect blame, then attack and reverse the victim and offender (DARVO), as previously discussed.

Now when we look at people pleasers, for example, we know that their behavioral patterns are also subconscious. There is also a very subtle manipulation happening below the people pleaser's level of awareness. When a people pleaser goes out of their way for someone else, it is with a hidden, underlying belief that if they meet someone else's needs first, then they will get their needs (for approval, love, recognition, attention, etc.) met in return, or alternatively it may help them avoid confrontation in some way. This type of manipulation does not harm or abuse other people, unlike the narcissist's manipulative behavior. The only person a people pleaser hurts is themselves (in case you needed another reminder)!

Could it be that a narcissist has a much stronger defense mechanism against pain, one that shields them from feeling the hurt they've caused? This defense may also prevent them from taking accountability for their actions. Is it possible they carry an overwhelming amount of shame that feels insurmountable to overcome, making it nearly impossible to accept responsibility? Remember, at their core, narcissists are deeply insecure. Or perhaps has their empathy gene (there is some evidence that there may be a genetic component to empathy!) been turned off through conditioning, their environment, or various other epigenetic factors?

A study by the University of Cambridge released in March 2018 found that "how empathetic we are is partly due to genetics"; however, genetics only account for 10 percent.[3] The remaining

---

3 "Study finds that genes play a role in empathy," University of Cambridge, March 12, 2018, https://www.cam.ac.uk/research/news/study-finds-that-genes-play-a-role-in-empathy.

factors that determine how much empathy we have are a result of our upbringing and our experiences. Nature versus nurture at its best.

Having a low level of empathy—something that can apply to anyone, not just narcissists—does not mean we are beyond repair, even if we experienced childhood trauma or were raised by parents who didn't consistently meet our needs. Empathy is a skill that can be developed, provided there is both the desire to grow and an awareness of its absence.

Some narcissists, for example, may be able to show empathy for animals, children, or those whom they deem inferior to them. They may even be able to express empathy toward someone who has no impact on their ego, status, or place on the pedestal.

Given that narcissists exhibit splitting—a black-and-white thinking pattern where individuals, situations, and experiences are either perceived as entirely good or entirely bad—they tend to categorize people as either valuable and superior or worthless and inferior.

This way of thinking is self-directed as well. If you, as the codependent in the relationship, gain too much power, money, intelligence, or status, then the narcissist may quickly devalue you out of fear that you'll upend them from the pedestal upon which they sit. They refuse to become the inferior one, and they certainly refuse to be made to feel as though they are not good enough because that hits a core wound. As a result, they attempt to increase their value by making you feel inferior. Or they may do this by exerting control over you, which makes them feel more powerful and, thus, superior.

So, What About Neuroplasticity and Epigenetics? Aren't We All Capable of Change?

Yes, we are all capable of change, but it requires two essential steps: first, recognizing the behavioral patterns that need to shift and, second, committing to the work of creating new neural pathways while healing past trauma.

Ultimately, we are only responsible for our own healing. We cannot compel anyone else to change or engage in the deep, transformative work necessary for growth. Change must be a personal choice, accompanied by a genuine willingness to fully commit to the process. While neuroplasticity allows us to rewire our neural pathways, this transformation is only possible when there is both awareness and acknowledgment of the thought and behavioral patterns that require disruption and reshaping.

This brings us back to our earlier question. *Is there any circumstance under which a narcissist is willing to change?* The short answer is that a narcissist will only change if they are deeply motivated to do so. However, meaningful change requires self-reflection and heightened self-awareness to identify the meanings, perceptions, and patterns that must be adjusted, reframed, or interrupted.

This process is especially challenging for narcissists, as their subconscious defense mechanisms were designed to shield them from pain. True healing requires *facing* and processing that pain, but biologically, our brains are wired to protect us from such discomfort. If the past emotional pain a narcissist has experienced is too overwhelming, their mind will instinctively work to deflect, reject, project, or distract them from facing it. While this tendency exists in all of us to some degree, narcissists often rely on more rigid and harmful avoidance strategies, making the process of change even more difficult for them.

While a narcissist may initially agree to therapy or couples counseling, once they are faced with revisiting painful past experiences or acknowledging their maladaptive traits, they may become overwhelmed and go running in the opposite direction. Admitting they are not as perfect as they believe themselves to be or, even more challenging, recognizing that someone in their past caused them significant harm requires them to confront feelings of weakness or vulnerability. This is something narcissists often avoid at all costs.

If they don't bolt out of the therapist's office, they may fall back into familiar patterns of deflecting blame onto others, such as the therapist or, even worse, you. This could not only perpetuate abusive behaviors but may even escalate them.

Before considering couples therapy with a narcissist, please carefully evaluate whether it will truly support your mental and emotional well-being. Participating in therapy with a narcissist could cause more harm than good. Instead, seeking out individual therapy or working with a trauma-informed coach who understands narcissistic abuse is often a more effective and supportive use of your time and resources. Prioritizing your own healing is the key to recovery and freedom.

Vulnerability is not something a narcissist embraces. To them, vulnerability signifies weakness, which they equate with inferiority. Due to their rigid thinking, they see themselves as either strong and exceptional or weak and worthless. This binary thinking extends to how they view others, including you, the codependent. In their eyes, you are either amazing and wonderful or worthless and inadequate. This is why the abuse cycle alternates between idealization and devaluation.

Back to Empathy...

Empathy is at the core of emotional connection and can be understood through two distinct forms: cognitive empathy and affective empathy.

Cognitive empathy is our ability to perceive and understand another person's thoughts and emotions. It's an intellectual grasp of what someone else is experiencing by putting yourself in someone else's shoes. Affective empathy, on the other hand, involves responding to those thoughts and feelings with an appropriate emotional reaction. It's the heartfelt, relational aspect of empathy that allows us to feel and connect with someone on a deeper level rather than simply understand them.

Both types of empathy rely on healthy emotional development, shaped by early relationships. Oxytocin, often referred to as the "love hormone," plays an important role in establishing social bonding and nurturing empathy. But what happens when a child grows up in an environment where empathy is absent?

Imagine a young child whose caregiver consistently dismisses their emotions, sending them to their room to calm down whenever they were angry or ignoring their distress. Without the caregiver modeling empathy or providing emotional support, the child lacks the oxytocin release needed to feel loved and connected. Over time, this child learns that emotions are not safe or acceptable, especially during moments of distress. This not only stifles their ability to feel loved but also prevents them from learning how to offer empathy to others. Instead, they might internalize shame for expressing "negative" emotions and develop patterns of emotional disconnection.

As the child grows, they may retain the ability to recognize others' emotions (cognitive empathy) but struggle to respond with compassion or appropriate emotional engagement (affective empathy). Compassion and sympathy are natural extensions of affective empathy, so without this foundation, they may feel disconnected and struggle to form emotional bonds. They may even become stuck in a freeze trauma response, dissociating from their feelings to protect themselves from the pain they've learned to suppress.

Empathy and Trauma: A Shared Struggle

For both narcissists and codependents, accessing empathy can be challenging if they have dissociated from their emotions due to childhood trauma. While the degree and nature of their experiences may differ, both have learned that their feelings are not safe to express. This survival strategy—dissociating to avoid pain—can cause patterns of emotional disconnection to persist into adulthood.

A narcissist may retain cognitive empathy, recognizing others' emotions, but struggle with affective empathy because responding with emotion would require confronting their own vulnerabilities. Similarly, a codependent might focus on "fixing" others while bypassing their own emotional needs, unable to fully connect on a deeper level. Both patterns reflect the same underlying difficulty: a fear of vulnerability and an instinctive avoidance of pain.

Vulnerability: The Key to Empathy

True empathy demands vulnerability—the willingness to feel another's emotions and allow those feelings to impact us. For both narcissists and codependents, this can feel overwhelming. Vulnerability threatens the protective walls they've built to avoid pain, exposing wounds they've worked hard to bury.

For the narcissist, their defense mechanisms are designed to avoid vulnerability—or, in their minds, weakness and inferiority—at all costs. Confronting their own emotional pain would mean acknowledging imperfection and facing unresolved wounds—a daunting prospect. For the codependent, vulnerability might manifest as fear of rejection or inadequacy. They may prioritize caring for others to earn love or approval while neglecting their own needs, afraid that addressing their emotions might make them appear selfish or unworthy.

This shared struggle with vulnerability points to a deeper issue: the lack of emotional safety necessary for growth. Without a foundation of internal security, both narcissists and codependents remain trapped in patterns that prevent them from accessing true empathy or meaningful healing. Understanding these patterns offers insight into how healing begins and why it can feel so elusive.

If parents failed to coregulate their children's nervous systems and teach them how to manage their emotions, the children may grow up feeling overwhelmed by their own feelings and those of others. Overwhelming emotions can lead to distress, which makes openness, vulnerability, and empathy feel unsafe or even threatening. To cope, the mind jumps in to protect them by suppressing emotions, avoiding pain, or using distractions to escape discomfort. Over time, their capacity for empathy diminishes because, on a subconscious level, they do not feel safe experiencing other people's emotions—especially when they don't even feel safe processing their own.

This emotional disconnect becomes a survival strategy that can pervade their adult relationships. For narcissists and codependents alike, the result is a shared struggle: the inability to access or fully express empathy. However, the ways in which this manifests—and the motivations behind it—differ significantly between the two.

While codependents prioritize connection and often overextend themselves to earn love or approval, narcissists operate from a place of self-preservation and control. Their engagement with others' emotions is often self-serving, designed to reinforce their sense of power or maintain the relationships that benefit them.

The key difference between a narcissist and a codependent lies in their focus: The codependent, while struggling with their own challenges, is not as self-centered as the narcissist. A narcissist may be capable of cognitive empathy—understanding how someone else feels—but their ability to access deeper, affective empathy is often limited. The empathy they do express rarely extends to admitting wrongdoing, showing genuine remorse, or taking accountability for causing emotional distress.

Even when a narcissist acknowledges how their actions made you feel, they are likely to justify their behavior and dismiss any harm caused. They may not see their behavior as abusive or unhealthy. Attempting to confront them about their behavior (which is not recommended due to potential safety risks) will likely lead them to accuse you of being dramatic or overly sensitive. In some cases, they may even gaslight you into believing that you are the abusive one or, worse, that you are the narcissist!

Narcissists can also exhibit seemingly empathetic behavior; however, as mentioned, their response may not make sense given the circumstances. For example, if your child becomes sick, forcing you to have to cancel your plans with the narcissist, they may initially ask about the child's well-being, appearing concerned. However, they may quickly shift to expressing frustration or anger about how the cancellation impacts them. This response reflects their inability to prioritize others' needs or emotions in a meaningful way. While sadness or concern for the sick child would be an appropriate emotional response, anger at the situation highlights the narcissist's self-centered perspective.

What's the Bottom Line?

Narcissists will only change if they are highly motivated to do so, and their willingness to change depends on whether the perceived outcome will benefit *them* in some way, not you.

They will not change *for* you, no matter how heartfelt your plea or how much they claim to love you. Instead, they may attempt to change to *keep* you, if they believe your presence enhances their status, value, or superiority. For example, if your partner sees you as someone who elevates them socially, financially, intellectually, or otherwise, they may put effort into maintaining the relationship.

Keep in mind, however, that narcissists have all-or-nothing thinking. People and situations are either entirely good or bad, valuable or worthless, idealized or devalued. If they believe that they are anything less than perfect, then they must be deeply flawed or inferior.

If your value to them lies in how you contribute to their image—whether by providing them with narcissistic supply, helping them maintain a facade, or enabling a lifestyle or status they feel entitled to—they might seem motivated to change if it means they can keep you.

However, any changes they make are likely to be superficial because true transformation requires vulnerability and self-reflection, two things narcissists typically avoid. Again, vulnerability equates to weakness and inferiority, while self-reflection forces them to confront parts of themselves they are trying desperately to hide, including feelings of deep insecurity. Facing this reality can feel like failure or evoke unbearable pain, so narcissists avoid it by maintaining their defenses. Instead of doing the deep inner work necessary for genuine change, they default to maladaptive coping strategies designed to protect themselves from discomfort.

This avoidance often results in a lack of self-awareness. Narcissists rarely believe anything is wrong with their behavior; instead, they are more likely to shift blame onto others—often you—or external circumstances. This deflection protects their fragile self-image but prevents meaningful growth.

Narcissistic behavior ultimately stems from extreme defense mechanisms built on judgment and criticism to feel worthy or "good enough." An overt narcissist tends to direct these criticism outwards, visibly blaming and devaluing others during the discard phase. A covert narcissist, however, may internalize this criticism, harshly judging themselves while subtly projecting those feelings onto their partner. Regardless of the type, the goal remains the same: to bolster their own sense of superiority or worth.

Mirror Neurons Versus Narcissistic Mirroring

All humans have mirror neurons. Mirror neurons help us learn as young babies and children to survive in this world. We observe our parents and caregivers to learn what is appropriate and what is not. Mirror neurons are the basis for empathy because they allow us to feel what other people are feeling or experiencing. They stimulate emotional recognition of what another might be feeling and then evoke a subsequent response subjective to one's own thoughts, experiences, and perceptions.

Think about when someone next to you yawns; you can't help but also yawn. That is an example of mirror neurons at work! Research has shown that people who identify as empaths have a high degree of mirror neurons, which is partly why they are able to deeply feel and empathize with what someone else is going through.

According to Leonard F. Häusser, "The discovery of mirror neurons allows a comprehension of empathy as an immediate and compassionate partaking of a response, enabling an understanding of the other person's feeling. At the same time, the resonating affect remains allocated to the other person, distinguishing this comprehensive process from a mere emotional contagion."[4]

Mirror neurons may be responsible for why empaths tend to absorb the emotions of others rather than discerning between which emotions are theirs and which emotions belong to others. Personally, once I understood how to discern the difference, I felt a lot less emotional and was able to then use my gift of empathy for the betterment of my relationships rather than allowing myself to get swept up into the emotional turbulence of others or the chaos of the abuse cycle.

My greatest piece of advice here is to practice being in your discernment of which emotions are yours and which are not. In order to do this, the first step is to be observant of how you are feeling before you step into a social situation or before interacting

---

[4] Leonard F. Häusser, "Empathie und Spiegelneurone. Ein Blick auf die Gegenwärtige Neuropsychologische Empathieforschung," [Empathy and Mirror Neurons. A View on Contemporary Neuropsychological Empathy Research], *Praxis der Kinderpsychologie und Kinderpsychiatrie* 61, no. 5 (2012): 322–35, https://doi.org/10.13109/prkk.2012.61.5.322.

with others. Once you are around others, notice how your emotional energy is impacted. If you are having a hard time discerning if what you are feeling is yours or not, then try to excuse yourself to a private space (your car, the bathroom, another room) where you can be alone for a minute or two. Then use the 2x breathing technique I explained previously until you feel safe and grounded. Place a hand on your heart and ask, either quietly or in your head, if this emotion is yours or not. I find that if the emotion dissipates and lifts quickly, then it is not mine. If it doesn't, then I know that the emotion is mine. I will then get curious and ask what the emotion is trying to share with me—what feels unsafe, what sensations are present, what wound has been poked? Our emotions are messengers to help us become aware of something that we may not be consciously aware of.

Mirror neurons may also be the reason some non-narcissistic partners begin to question whether they, too, are narcissists. They may begin to first question this because the narcissist has projected and made claims that their partner is the narcissist, not them. But remember that there are some similarities between codependents and narcissists which could account for why someone who is not a narcissist may begin to question if they are.

The other factor is that sometimes, after years of being in a relationship with a narcissist, the non-narcissistic partner may adapt some of the narcissistic behaviors because it is how they have learned to stay safe in the relationship. Through mirror neurons, they learn how to manipulate in order to potentially maintain some semblance of control or get their needs met.

I find that children of a narcissistic parent often question whether both of their parents are narcissists due to some of the mirroring that happens within the long-term relationship. While I do not have enough data to support any hard facts, I believe that likely one parent is the narcissist and over time, the codependent parent learned to mirror the narcissist's behaviors in order to minimize the abuse inflicted on them by the narcissist. Remember, narcissists prefer that others are like them because then they will not be a threat. As long as the narcissist continues to maintain the control and upper hand and feel superior, then they will not discard the codependent partner, whose biggest fear is being abandoned. This fear motivates the codependent partner to behave in ways that will maintain the security of the relationship, even if it means hurting themselves or others.

Back to mirror neurons: There is currently a lot of scientific research being done that is exploring the relationship between narcissism and mirror neurons. While the research is still out as to whether narcissists actually have a lower number of mirror neurons than those of us who aren't narcissists, there have been studies that show how there may be other brain structure impairments exemplifying why a narcissist may be able to feel and express sufficient cognitive empathy but not affective empathy.[5]

What About Narcissistic Mirroring? What Is It and How Is It Different?

Narcissistic mirroring differs significantly from the natural role of mirror neurons in healthy relationships. While mirror neurons help us empathize and connect by reflecting others' emotions and experiences, narcissistic mirroring is a deliberate tactic designed to manipulate rather than foster genuine connection.

At first, narcissistic mirroring can make the narcissist seem genuinely empathetic, as they appear to share your likes, reflect your feelings, or bond with you over a common experience. However, the intentions and motivations are not altruistic. Narcissists use this behavior to create a false sense of emotional safety and familiarity, lulling you into trusting them. Once you feel deeply understood and seen, they exploit your vulnerability for their gain.

This tactic stems from the narcissist's fragile sense of self. Since they lack a stable identity, they mirror others to secure acceptance and admiration. While this behavior may not always be premeditated, a malignant, sadistic narcissist might consciously and methodically mirror your behaviors, preferences, and even past

---

5 Arielle Baskin-Sommers et al., "Empathy in Narcissistic Personality Disorder: From Clinical and Empirical Perspectives," *Personality Disorders* 5, no. 3 (2014): 323–33, https://doi.org/10.1037/per0000061; Kamila Jankowiak-Siuda and Wojciech Zajkowski, "A Neural Model of Mechanisms of Empathy Deficits in Narcissism," *Medical Science Monitor: International Medical Journal of Experimental and Clinical Research* 19 (2013): 934–41, https://doi.org/10.12659/MSM.889593.

experiences. This deliberate form of mirroring is meant to reinforce a sense of comfort and belonging, making it easier for them to maintain control and manipulate you.

Understanding narcissistic mirroring is crucial. While mirror neurons in healthy relationships facilitate learning, connection, and empathy, narcissistic mirroring weaponizes these same processes for selfish ends. Recognizing this behavior can help you maintain boundaries and protect yourself from emotional manipulation.

If the Narcissist Has Apologized, Doesn't That Mean They Are Changing?

When a narcissist apologizes, it's essential to consider the nature and intent behind their words or actions. Did they clearly admit to any wrongdoing? Did they take genuine responsibility for their actions, or was the apology vague and performative?

In many cases, a narcissist's apology takes the form of gestures rather than sincere accountability. They might offer grand displays of remorse, such as expensive gifts or dramatic acts, or subtler efforts like buying dinner or temporarily helping around the house. While these gestures may include the words "I'm sorry," they are often intended to placate you and maintain control rather than address the harm caused.

A genuine apology involves acknowledging your feelings, understanding what went wrong, and taking accountability. It also provides an opportunity to rebuild trust by discussing how to prevent similar issues in the future. In healthy relationships, this process creates connection and mutual respect. However, with a narcissist, apologies are often one-sided and insincere. If you admit fault first, they may seize the opportunity to absolve themselves entirely, shifting the emotional burden onto you.

Be aware of empty or manipulative apologies. Narcissists often use apologies as a tool to shift focus onto you, prompting you to admit wrongdoing, while they avoid any of the blame. These apologies may aim to maintain their control over the relationship rather than repair the harm caused.

Relationships take two; however, being with a narcissist often feels unbalanced. You may find yourself carrying the emotional labor, the blame, and the responsibility for maintaining the connection. Narcissists frequently use tactics like blame shifting and DARVO (deny, attack, and reverse victim and offender) to keep themselves in a position of power while leaving you feeling unsupported and alone.

If you are constantly the one apologizing, you are giving the narcissist the upper hand. It allows them to stay in control, keeping you in a cycle where you shoulder the emotional weight of the relationship while they avoid accountability. Recognizing these patterns is a vital step toward reclaiming your emotional well-being and establishing healthier boundaries.

Are People Pleasers Covert Narcissists?

If you've ever wondered if you are, in fact, a narcissist, then there is a likely chance that you are not a narcissist. Phew, right!?

Before we jump in, let's define the term "people pleaser." A people pleaser is someone who compromises their authenticity, time, value, or energy in order to meet the needs of others before their own. Their sense of self-worth is supported by the recognition and attention they receive for helping others. People pleasers often feel responsible for other people's emotions and, as such, will do all they can to keep the people around them happy, even if it means self-sacrificing or self-abandoning their needs, wants, and desires. All people pleasers are codependents; however, not all codependents are people pleasers.

As we mentioned before, people pleasing is both a trauma or stress response called fawning and a coping mechanism, or protector part, of codependents. With people pleasing, a subtle manipulation is happening: If I appease you, you will accept, value, or love me, and as a result, I will stay safe. This manipulation may be entirely subconscious, just like the narcissist's behavior may be subconscious. Each is just trying to get their needs met; so, is the people pleaser a covert narcissist?

The answer is no. The people pleaser, unless they are stuck in a freeze response and are completely dissociated, will have a high degree of emotional intelligence and empathy. They are typically very empathic and can tune into the moods and emotions of those around them, which is partly why they feel responsible for other people's emotions. They often believe they are the reason someone is upset and may easily absorb the emotions of others around them. Ultimately, the people pleaser is only truly hurting themselves, not anyone else, which is a huge differentiating factor because narcissists hurt others with their behavior, never themselves.

Should We Be Labeling Narcissists, Codependents, or People Pleasers?

As mentioned, all people pleasers are codependent, as are all narcissists. So, does that mean we can then draw the conclusion that people pleasers are also narcissists? The short answer is no and while we have already addressed this previously, I think it might be helpful to explore it a bit further to help put you at ease.

First, as you know, narcissists usually have a low amount or lack of empathy. People pleasers, on the other hand, have a much higher degree of empathy. However, when we look at what creates a narcissist and what creates a people pleaser, it's the exact same thing. Both have experienced some kind of childhood trauma and as a result, have developed unhealthy coping mechanisms.

They have developed these coping strategies subconsciously (unless they are malignant narcissists, in which case they are more calculated and consciously hurt others) to get their needs met.

What are the needs of a people pleaser and a narcissist? At their core, they have the same needs as everyone else: to feel loved and to belong. As human beings, we are all wired for connection.

For a people pleaser, the greatest fear is abandonment. For a narcissist, the greatest fear is rejection. Fundamentally, these fears are the same: a fear of not belonging. Both are driven by a deep-seated fear of disconnection, manifesting in different ways but rooted in the same core need.

The coping mechanisms they've developed to get their needs met are subconscious, as we've discussed. However, both the people pleaser and the narcissist are manipulative in their own way. The people pleaser's manipulation comes in the form of self-sacrifice: "If I behave a certain way, or achieve something significant, do more for others, or give more to others, then I will be seen as important, lovable, worthy, or enough." Their actions are driven by a subconscious belief that their value lies in what they do for others, often at the expense of their own well-being.

The narcissist, on the other hand, manipulates by exploiting and often hurting others to feel important, lovable, worthy, or enough. While the people pleaser primarily harms themselves through self-abandonment, self-sacrifice, and settling for far less than they deserve, the narcissist directs their harm outward. They erode others' self-worth, self-esteem, and self-trust in an effort to elevate their own sense of value, lovability, or enough-ness.

It's important to recognize that labeling individuals as narcissists, people pleasers, or codependents can feel unfair, as these behaviors and traits often develop as coping mechanisms in response to childhood trauma or adverse childhood experiences (ACEs). These adaptations were strategies to feel safe in the world, not inherent flaws. The labels, however, can be a useful, succinct way of alluding to certain subconscious behaviors and traits that have arisen from childhood trauma. When used thoughtfully, they provide a framework for understanding patterns rather than defining someone's identity.

By reframing these labels as tools for discussion rather than judgment, we can begin to view one another as humans carrying our own unique trauma-induced wounds. This perspective allows us to approach one another through a trauma-informed lens with compassion, empathy, love, and understanding.

When we continue to villainize and blame the narcissist, we inadvertently trap ourselves in the Karpman Drama Triangle of codependency, cycling between the roles of victim, rescuer, and persecutor. This keeps us disempowered, stuck in the mindset of a victim, rather than stepping into the role of an empowered thriver. True growth begins when we learn how to love and accept ourselves, even with our wounds and maladaptive patterns. From this place of self-acceptance, we can extend compassion and understanding for others who are also navigating their own wounds and coping mechanisms.

Boundaries are essential in this process. They allow us to accept others for who they are while maintaining healthy limits around the way we deserve to be treated. Abuse is abuse and there is no excuse. Just because you accept the narcissist for who they are and may be able to offer them compassion and understanding does not mean you should tolerate any harmful behavior. By communicating and affirming our boundaries, we engage in powerful acts of self-love. Boundaries serve as tools for fostering safe vulnerability, deeper understanding, and mutual respect in healthy relationships.

However, setting boundaries with a narcissist presents unique challenges, as they often resist or disregard those limits. It remains your responsibility to consistently reinforce and remind them of your boundaries. While this may feel exhausting, it is a critical step in reclaiming your power and protecting your emotional well-being.

Remember, boundaries are not about controlling the other person; they are about honoring yourself. By prioritizing your needs and affirming your worth, you model self-respect and create the foundation for establishing healthier, more balanced relationships in the future. We'll dive more into boundaries in chapter ten.

What Are the Childhood Wounds That Are Inflicted?

Interestingly enough, the wounds of the narcissist and the codependent are very similar. What makes them different are the traits, behaviors, and tactics they use in order to heal and soothe those wounds.

They each will struggle with not feeling lovable, worthy, enough, or important unless _____ (fill in the blank). That blank could be unless *I am performing, earning, adored, center of attention, succeeding, perfect, in control, attaining, acquiring, achieving, or better than XYZ.*

When we stop having to validate ourselves through other people or our relationships, or when we stop chasing the love we seek that we cannot give ourselves from other people, and heal those wounds within us, *then* we can change, and *then* we can all heal.

While it has been said that narcissists cannot change for various reasons and while we have discussed whether it's possible in this book, we cannot say with any conviction or merit that it is true in the absolute.

It is, however, true that we cannot change what we do not acknowledge or accept. That applies to anyone, whether you are a narcissist, a victim of narcissistic abuse, or Jane Smith.

Victims—a word I'd rather not use, but for lack of a better word—are not going to change unless they become aware of how they are being hurt in the relationship. Sometimes, the behaviors and tactics are so subtle they may not even be aware that what they are experiencing is, in fact, emotional or psychological abuse. It's possible they may even make excuses for their partner's, parent's, or boss's behavior rather than recognize the damage being done to their self-worth, self-confidence, and overall emotional well-being. It may feel too uncomfortable, vulnerable, embarrassing, or scary to admit that this insidious form of abuse is even occurring.

It's not until we have awareness of being hurt that we're able to make a change and do something different.

A significant part of the healing journey involves addressing the wounds caused by childhood trauma. These wounds may stem from having a narcissistic parent or an emotionally negligent or avoidant caregiver. When a child's emotional needs are unmet or when they learn that love is conditional, painful, or something that has to be earned, they may not recognize these experiences as a form of emotional abuse. In some cases, this wounding may include physical abuse.

Healing begins with understanding and acknowledging the impact of these early experiences, allowing space for self-compassion and growth. Over time, awareness and deep healing can lead to a place of acceptance, where we may find it possible to forgive our parents or caregivers, recognizing that they were only acting with the limited awareness they had at the time. We may also begin to see that their behaviors stemmed from their own deep inner wounds and insecurities—wounds they may still carry and act upon today.

Trauma literally changes the way our genes express themselves, and that modification can be passed down to us from our great-great-great-great-great grandparents through epigenetics. Research has shown trauma can be passed down up to seven generations, with other studies claiming it can be passed down through as few as four generations to as many as fourteen generations.[6]

If we are able to forgive and accept our parents for the hurt they may have caused, then can we also learn to forgive the narcissist? Can we learn to forgive ourselves?

If we forgave all the people in our lives who have hurt us and forgive ourselves as well because we also had a role in perpetuating certain maladaptive behavioral patterns that kept the cycles of abuse in place, could we disrupt the pattern of generational trauma for future generations?

If a narcissist *never* takes accountability for their actions, and as the survivor, you avoid reflecting on how you ended up in the relationship and the patterns that allowed it to continue, the cycle of hurt will persist. Without accountability and self-awareness on all sides, we remain hurt people who unintentionally perpetuate harm.

The truth is, you're not responsible for someone else's actions, but you *are* responsible for own. You're not responsible for how others' feel, but you *are* responsible for managing your own emotions. You're not responsible for healing other people, but you *are* responsible for your own healing.

Healing from trauma requires us to step away from labeling and judging others because our judgment often mirrors the harsh inner dialogue that we direct at ourselves. When we allow our inner critic to dominate, we stifle our ability to offer self-compassion and empathy.

By learning to quiet our inner critic and fully love and accept ourselves, we free ourselves from self-judgment. In doing so, we also stop judging those around us. When we can embrace our imperfections and recognize that it's okay to be human, we create space to accept others, imperfections and all.

---

[6] "What is Epigenetics?," MedlinePlus, U.S. Department of Health and Human Services, updated June 11, 2021, https://medlineplus.gov/genetics/understanding/howgeneswork/epigenome/.
Trauma—specifically generational trauma—is being studied for its effects on genetics. Epigenetics is the study of heritable changes in gene function that occur without alterations to the DNA sequence. These changes involve chemical modifications to DNA and associated proteins that regulate gene expression, influencing how genes are turned on or off.

This acceptance is where true inner peace begins. It's in knowing that we can fill ourselves with so much love that it overflows, allowing us to share it generously and unconditionally.

When we connect to the universal source of love, we can give freely without prejudice, judgment, or criticism. We don't need to decide who is worthy of our love, because as human beings, we are all inherently worthy.

While we may be misguided at times and act out from our own hurt and trauma, we also need to forgive ourselves because we are all works in progress. As the saying goes, healing is not a destination but a lifelong journey. None of us can truly heal if we remain stuck in labeling, criticizing, and judging others and, thereby, ourselves.

The only way forward is to increase your own awareness, work with your body to somatically release the trauma, learn to open your heart vulnerably to love and accept yourself first, and then generously bestow it upon others. Of course, it is easier said than done and it requires conscious effort and intentional action, but it is most certainly possible!

A footnote on forgiveness: Forgiveness is for *you* so you can feel at peace. It is not for the other person. You don't even have to tell the toxic people in your life that you have forgiven them. It also does not mean you have to forget what happened or allow them back into your life in an intimate way, nor does it mean you should tolerate or accept behavior that is hurtful or toxic. It just means you are able to forgive what has happened because you understand how they may have been acting out their hurt. That doesn't make their actions okay or acceptable, but you forgive them because you can see they are human, too, with the same invisible wounds.

Chapter Eleven

THE GOLDEN CHILD, THE SCAPEGOAT, AND THE CAREGIVER ALL WALK INTO A BAR

The role a child ends up playing within the family home can impact how they show up in their relationships as an adult. It can also create an interconnected pattern of unhealthy behaviors as a way to earn acceptance, recognition, attention, and love when dysfunctional family dynamics are present.

The Golden Child

The golden child is the child who can do no wrong, and who is put up on a pedestal and adored for all the things they achieve, earn, do, etc. Typically, this child will be highly intelligent, talented, or skilled, which earns them this recognition, and which the unhealthy parent often will see as a reflection of themselves. This can put a lot of pressure on the child to constantly perform, achieve, or behave in a way that will win their parents' approval, adoration, love, or recognition.

The golden child may be above reproach and shielded from experiencing any type of discipline or consequences as a result of their "golden" status. Other children within the family may be compared to the golden child, leaving them feeling as though they could never measure up or be enough in the eyes of their parents.

One or both parents may go out of their way to shield the golden child from any negative aspects within the family home. For example, if one parent has a substance abuse problem, the golden child may be highly protected—or at least a great attempt will be made to protect them—from the erratic or inflammatory behavior of the dependent parent. The golden child may also be the codependent parent's pride and joy with the focus and attention placed on them as a way to, number one, make the codependent parent feel worthy and validated as a parent and, number two, distract others within their social circles, as well as themselves, from the unhealthy environment that exists at home with the dependent parent.

As a result, the golden child may grow up with a sense of entitlement, be unable to take accountability for their actions, and expect special treatment from every person they encounter, whether from their future spouse or the poor customer service agent who's answered their call. This can contribute to narcissistic traits, as the golden child may struggle with empathy and have difficulty recognizing others' needs since their own needs and emotions were prioritized in the family home—above those of the codependent parent and siblings.

The Scapegoat

The scapegoat is the opposite of the golden child. This child can do nothing right. They often bear the brunt of the family's shortcoming, mistakes, or wrongdoings, essentially becoming the "cause" of the family's dysfunction. They will be the first to be blamed when something goes wrong. This is the child who is automatically assumed to have done something wrong whenever there is conflict among the children or even between the scapegoat and the other parent.

Sadly, the scapegoat often becomes the target of the family's frustrations. This could even ripple out into extended family dynamics as well, where the scapegoat is blamed and shamed for being the difficult or naughty one, for example.

The scapegoat may be very outspoken and defensive and could grow up with very low self-esteem and little to no self-worth. They may subconsciously feel rejected, unwanted, unloved, and as though nothing they do is ever good enough.

Outwardly, they may display rebellious or defiant behaviors and never take accountability for their actions as a result of having been wrongly accused of things they didn't do during childhood. It can feel safer for the scapegoat to deflect responsibility for their actions because their deep sense of shame feels too overwhelming to admit any wrongdoing.

The scapegoat may also struggle with empathy, especially if it was not ever modeled for them by their parents. Instead of showing concern, understanding, or compassion, the parents may have just blamed them for everything, leaving their emotional needs unmet and creating a sense of disconnection.

As a result, the scapegoat is at risk for developing codependent tendencies and potentially narcissistic behaviors. Remember, a high degree of narcissists are codependent, but not all codependents are narcissists.

The Lost Child

The lost child is neither the golden child nor the scapegoat, both of which take up the majority of the family's attention. The lost child will deeply crave the love and attention of others and may feel lonely, isolated, and misunderstood.

This child may become emotionally distant and withdraw in relationships. They will struggle to ask for what they need or disallow support or care as they have become used to being small, not taking up too much space. They will do what they can to avoid conflict by minimizing how they feel, what they need, or how they've been hurt in order to not rock the boat.

It's possible the lost child may create their own imaginary world or imaginary friends as a coping mechanism. They will grow up feeling out of place, as if they don't belong, or not having a strong sense of who they are.

The lost child may also manifest real or feigned illnesses as a way to receive empathy, love, and attention that they do not receive on a regular basis. Real illnesses may arise entirely on a subconscious level.

As they mature, they may struggle to express their emotions and form connections. Their avoidance can lead to codependent tendencies where they continually seek external validation and approval.

The Caretaker/Parentified Child

The caretaker ends up taking on responsibility beyond their age, becoming the surrogate parent for their siblings and, potentially, their parents. This child often puts the needs of everyone else above their own and becomes a people pleaser who prioritizes everyone else's happiness. They may be the caretaker of the entire family or just one family member in particular.

This child will struggle with boundaries and prioritizing their own needs. As a result, they may seek out the approval and validation of others and easily make excuses for others' bad behavior. Consequently, they may have difficulty coping with others' disappointment, especially if directed toward them.

Since they have been commended so often for being mature beyond their years, they may grow up feeling as though they have to be responsible all the time, leading to a life of hyper-independence and taking more responsibility in their relationships than they should. This could contribute to repressed anger and deep underlying resentment in their partnerships later in life.

As you may guess, the caretaker is primed for codependency because of their struggle with setting boundaries, asking for what they need and over-responsibility for others. They will find it difficult to ask for help or prioritize their own well-being.

The Mascot/Clown

The mascot is the family clown: the child who uses humor or light heartedness as a way to soften or distract from the family's problems. This child will take on the responsibility of lightening the mood when things become too intense and as a way to mask the family's dysfunction.

This child will be hypervigilant—constantly scanning the room and the emotions of all present—in case they have to alter the atmosphere. If things feel too serious or the family tensions become too palpable, the mascot will jump in to shake things up with playfulness and comedy to take the focus off the uneasiness brewing beneath the surface. They may be viewed as the peacekeeper as well; however, where the peacekeeper will try to resolve the issues, the mascot does their best to sweep things under the rug.

As a result, the mascot may struggle to take things seriously and avoid dealing with deeper emotions. This coping strategy may lead to codependency as they focus on managing other people's emotions and keeping the peace rather than addressing underlying issues or feeling their own emotions. At times, their difficulty with emotional connection and tendency to sweep problems under the rug may create the appearance of self-focused behaviors. They often rely on hypervigilance, humor, and charm to deflect from deeper issues in relationships, not out of manipulation, but as a subconscious way to avoid conflict and maintain stability.

The Peacekeeper/Mediator

The peacekeeper or mediator is the one who constantly tries to negotiate peace among family members. This often comes at the cost of getting their own needs met because they are more concerned about making sure everyone else is happy and getting along. They may also be dragged into conflict to mediate between two arguing family members.

The peacemaker may struggle to know what their needs are and ask for what they need in their relationships. They will self-abandon and self-sacrifice as a way to avoid confrontation at all costs, thereby minimizing their wants, needs, desires, or concerns. They likely will not have strong opinions or beliefs as they may have been conditioned to believe that having strong beliefs or opinions leads to conflict.

On the outside, the peacekeeper may seem easy going and laid back since they will do all they can to avoid conflict; however, over time, they may experience resentment and anger that their feelings, needs, wants, or desires are never considered. The irony is that this is *because* the peacemaker will avoid speaking their truth out of the fear of confrontation. The peacemaker may be deeply empathic and might use their gift of empathy as a weapon against themselves in order to stay safe.

This child will also grow up to be hypervigilant like the mascot, gauging the emotional energy of the room so they can jump in to help maintain the peace or walk out of a room if the tension feels overwhelming. They are often very good at minimizing their own feelings and making excuses for other people's poor behavior as a way to smooth things over. They often take on excessive responsibility, apologizing and accepting blame even when they are not at fault in an effort to preserve harmony in their relationships.

Since the peacemaker is more likely to self-abandon and self-sacrifice their own needs as a way to keep the peace, they will be highly susceptible to codependent relationships as well.

The role of peacekeeper can feel utterly exhausting if there is a high degree of dysfunction in the childhood home, as refereeing all the family quarrels and conflicts in order to restore homeostasis to the family home can be draining.

Reflections

With all of these roles, it is important to note that none of them are mutually exclusive. They all represent different coping mechanisms that children will adopt at different times. So, if you identified with more than one role mentioned above, that is typical. It is possible that you may have played one role more predominantly with one family member and another with others, for example. Alternatively, you may have played multiple roles within your family dynamic and in your adult relationships.

It's important to mention that not all children in a dysfunctional family will develop narcissistic or codependent traits as it depends on their individual resilience (their nervous systems), their attachment style, and the amount of support they receive, either from within or outside of the family dynamic.

Understanding these dynamics, however, can prove to be very beneficial in breaking the cycle of dysfunctional family relational patterns. It is also helpful to understand the role your partner or loved one may have played in their family dynamic growing up as it can provide you with more insight into why they behave the way they do. Reflecting on your children's roles within your family may also be helpful, if you are a parent. With awareness and understanding, healing and growth is possible across generations!

Chapter Twelve

THE ROLES OF ATTACHMENT WOUNDS

You may already be familiar with attachment styles, or maybe you've never heard of them before. They are important to understand because our attachment styles are responsible for how we relate to other people and the basis upon which we build the foundations of our relationships.

British psychologist John Bowlby created the key concepts in attachment theory. He described attachment as a "lasting psychological connectedness between human beings."[7] Bowlby posited that the initial attachments children develop with their caregivers profoundly influence their psychological development and relationships throughout their entire lives.

Attachment theory emphasizes that when primary caregivers are consistently available and responsive to an infant's needs, the child feels secure. This reliability fosters a dependable relationship, enabling the child to confidently explore their surroundings.

Therefore, our attachment styles are formed within the first eighteen months of childhood. When we are first born, the relationship we have with our primary caregiver becomes the basis for how we learn to attach to others.

If you are a parent, you may wish to also think about this from your child's perspective to understand their attachment style as well.

---

7 John Bowlby, *Attachment and Loss*, vol. 1, *Attachment* (Hogarth Press, 1969).

Overall, your attachment style will be heavily influenced by your caregiver's attachment style or potentially by how they have been conditioned to mother and nurture. Before we dive deeper, let's identify the four attachment styles.

The four attachment styles are secure, anxious, avoidant, and disorganized. Some therapists may identify the four attachments styles slightly differently, so you may have heard them described as secure, anxious, anxious avoidant, and fearful avoidant. There are other variations as well; however, I personally prefer to use the four names that are easily distinguishable rather than confusing you with descriptions that are different combinations of the same words.

Secure Attachment

Secure attachment is the kind of attachment we all yearn for and hope to have with our children and partners. Individuals with secure attachment typically had a caregiver or parent who responded consistently to their needs as a child. For example, if the child was crying, the parent would soothe, comfort, and meet the needs of the child in an attentive manner. As a result, the child would come to expect that if they were in distress or were struggling in some fashion, their parent or caregiver would respond in the appropriate way without causing unreasonable stress. This allows the child to build trust in the caregiver. They learn when they are in distress, the caregiver will reliably meet their needs most of the time.

This type of attachment creates a strong bond between the child and their parent and establishes a solid foundation for emotional security and healthy relationships. This securely attached individual is able to take accountability in their relationships as well as place appropriate responsibility on their partners for their actions. Someone who is securely attached does not assign meaning to themselves if the relationship succeeds or fails. A securely attached individual is more often able to create interdependent relationships with other securely attached individuals.

While this attachment style seems almost unattainable to those who have experienced narcissistic trauma, know that it is possible to learn how to securely attach to others in a healthy way once you recover from the trauma. This is not to say that a relationship where there is a secure attachment is perfect, as you may still find yourself triggered and you may have moments of insecurity, conflict, etc. This is all normal. You are human and none of us is perfect. Understand that this is the type of attachment we are all striving for.

Anxious Attachment

Anxious attachment is where a parent or caregiver inconsistently met the needs of the child, leaving the child feeling insecure about whether their needs would be met in times of struggle or distress. As a result, these children grow up with a fear of abandonment and a heightened need for reassurance and validation. They grow up to become adults who rely excessively on their partners for validation, approval, recognition, love, and constant reassurance. These individuals are often clingy in relationships and may end up chasing, self-sacrificing, or people pleasing their partner in order to get them to stay in the relationship. When the relationship ends, the anxiously attached individual may blame themselves for the failed relationship and believe that they did something wrong or that the relationship failed because they are not good enough. They may wonder what else they could have done to keep the relationship going. Likely, they will struggle with self-confidence and self-esteem and have a strong inner critic.

Someone with an anxious attachment may also find that they often take over-responsibility in the relationship's survival which is driven by their fear of abandonment.

Avoidant Attachment

Avoidant attachment is where a parent or caregiver was either emotionally distant or unresponsive to the child's needs. As a result, children who grow up with avoidant attachment tend to become less reliant on others to meet their needs and may avoid emotional intimacy at all costs because they have learned it is safer to not rely on others. They may struggle with trust issues, emotional expression, and vulnerability. Those with avoidant attachment may resist commitment or be the partner who runs when things get a little too intimate or when someone gets a little too close emotionally. They are more often the partner who ends the relationship and may come off as seeming devoid of all emotion.

Someone with avoidant attachment may walk away the minute things feel hard or if they feel that something is no longer perfect. They can have a strong perfectionist part and may run at the first hint of disharmony, as they anticipate hurt, disappointment, or—worst of all—rejection from their partner. Rejection is the avoidant's biggest fear, and as a result, they'd rather reject someone first than wait around to be dumped.

Disorganized Attachment

Disorganized attachment is a combination of both anxious and avoidant attachment styles. This person's parent or caregiver may have been inconsistently responsive or unresponsive. Oftentimes, individuals with disorganized attachment grew up in homes where there was emotional neglect or abuse. Recognizing disorganized attachment is important for trauma recovery. If this is your predominant attachment style, it will be very helpful to focus your learning on how to create safety within yourself and, subsequently, your relationships by processing your trauma. In processing your trauma and working to release it from your body, you will be able to create healthier coping mechanisms and disrupt the patterns created as a result of your early childhood experiences. This is, of course, true for all the attachment styles, except for secure attachment.

A person with disorganized attachment may run very hot and very cold. There will be a lot of chaos and drama in their relationships as a result. They may push people away out of a fear of rejection, only to then smother them again once they feel like the fear of rejection has passed and the fear of abandonment kicks in.

Each of the attachment styles has been presented in its most distinct or pure form to illustrate core characteristics, but in reality, each style can be more nuanced and layered. Many people see aspects of themselves in more than one attachment style, especially since these patterns can shift with time, personal growth, and new experiences. This natural fluidity in our attachment patterns reflects the complexity of our journeys and the unique ways we relate to others.

For example, it is not entirely uncommon for someone who has experienced narcissistic abuse to observe that when they were younger, they identified as someone who was anxiously attached. After a series of toxic and unhealthy relationships, they may feel they became more avoidantly attached or perhaps over time, more disorganized.

When we are healing our attachment wounds, it's fairly typical to end up swinging to the opposite side of the spectrum. For example, if you initially had an anxious attachment style, you might find yourself developing avoidant tendencies in later relationships as part of the healing process. Over time, with deep inner work, the hope is to end up somewhere back in the middle, closer to having a secure attachment style.

The reason for identifying your primary attachment style is not to necessarily box you into one type, but rather to help you better understand the relational dynamics that have shaped your experiences and to become aware of your emotional responses. When you have more awareness of your patterns and dynamics, you are able to get curious when these patterns arise. With curiosity, you can delve deeper into understanding your patterns and why they were created. It is then with understanding and acceptance that we are able to disrupt the subconscious patterning, alter our emotional responses, and create healthier coping mechanisms.

When we understand our attachment style, we can make more informed decisions in our relationships, allowing us to choose healthier partners and situations that align with our growth and recovery. It helps us to understand what our attachment wounds may be and how we may be acting from them inside of our relationships when we feel triggered or perceive a threat or danger.

If we look back at parents' and grandparents' attachment styles, we can see that often, our attachment style is a product of generational trauma since our parents' attachment styles heavily influenced our own. In order to break free of generational patterns, we must become aware of our own patterns so we can intentionally change how we approach and engage in our relationships. It can also help us create healthier attachment styles with our children.

Being a cycle breaker brings a lot of responsibility, and it can feel, at times, like we are doing a lot of heavy lifting. Know that you are healing unhealthy patterns not only for yourself but also for your children and future generations. There is great purpose in doing the deep, inner work, and while there is no destination you need to reach, every step you take forward helps to create healthier and more meaningful connections with others.

Chapter Thirteen

Symptoms of Narcissistic Abuse

Narcissistic abuse often happens below our level of awareness. We may recognize we are unhappy in the relationship but not quite understand that we may also be experiencing the symptoms of the abuse as well.

Below is a list of emotional, psychological, mental, and physical symptoms. Which ones resonate with you?

Emotional Symptoms
- Anxiety
- Depression
- Shame and guilt
- Low self-esteem
- Feeling worthless
- Feeling powerless and helpless
- Feeling stuck or trapped
- Self-blame and self-criticism

Psychological Symptoms
- Dissociation
- Self-doubt and second-guessing
- Difficulty concentrating
- Forgetfulness and memory issues
- Obsessive thinking about abuser

Mental Symptoms
- Brain fog
- Confusion

- Indecisiveness

Physical Symptoms
- Chronic pain
- Tension in body
- Chronic fatigue and exhaustion
- Sleep disturbances and insomnia
- Digestive and stomach issues
- Headaches and migraines
- High blood pressure
- Heart palpitations
- Weakened immune system
- Autoimmune issues

The symptoms of narcissistic abuse manifest as a result of complex neurophysiological processes that are impacted by the body's response to chronic stress and trauma. In order to better understand what happens in the body, we will need to discuss the neurobiological connection of the brain, the nervous system, and the endocrine system.

While this book is not intended to dive deep into an exploration of the brain, the nervous system, and the endocrine system, I am going to do my best to at least give you a cursory understanding so you can begin to appreciate just how amazing your body is and how it's always working hard to keep you safe.

Please also note that if you are experiencing any of the symptoms above, it is important to seek professional medical attention and not dismiss them. While narcissistic abuse *may* help explain why you are experiencing these symptoms, your health is of the utmost importance, and being seen by a medical doctor is imperative to your well-being.

Impact of Trauma

When your nervous system is triggered into a fight or flight response, which is a sympathetic nervous system state, it's because the amygdala in your brain has detected some kind of threat or danger.

That threat or danger may be real (as in your life is truly at stake) or it may just be that the amygdala perceives the threat is going to cause deep, emotional, or spiritual pain based on the perception of a past experience, as discussed in chapter ten.

After experiencing trauma, the amygdala can become hypersensitive and perceive danger everywhere, keeping you stuck in a fight or flight response or if the threat is more dangerous, a freeze response.

Your ability to recall information or remember certain details may also be difficult after experiencing trauma as the hippocampus, the brain's file cabinet, becomes impacted. This can lead to forgetfulness or not being able to remember the chronological order of events, details of a conversation, or memories correctly.

The prefrontal cortex is the part of the brain responsible for executive function, rational thinking, and logic. When the prefrontal cortex is impacted by trauma, you may struggle to focus, make clear decisions, regulate your emotions, or think clearly. You may also suffer from brain fog, doubt, and confusion.

When the amygdala perceives danger, neurotransmitters are sent to the HPA (hypothalamus-pituitary-adrenal) axis as previously explained, which then triggers your nervous system into fight or flight or, if the threat persists, into a freeze response.

The hypothalamus regulates breathing, metabolism, and digestion, and in response to trauma, it will increase our breathing rate and slow down our metabolism and digestion because the last thing we need to feel while fighting or fleeing for our life is hunger, thirst, or the need to go to the bathroom.

The adrenal glands first secrete adrenaline, providing a rush of energy and an increased blood flow to oxygenate your extremities so you can either run toward the threat to fight or run away from it to flee. The adrenals then secrete cortisol to keep you on high alert to look out for the next threat.

When you remain in a state of hypervigilance for an extended period of time due to trauma, your body is constantly being flooded with stress hormones and, in particular, cortisol. We know that when the body is being flooded by cortisol, it increases inflammation. And increased inflammation leads to disease, chronic pain, and even cancer. Prolonged activation of a fight or flight response (elevated cortisol levels) can also lead to increased anxiety and panic attacks.

When we are stuck in fight or flight due to trauma, it can cause other health issues as well. Our digestion slows down, our sleeping patterns get out of whack, and we become less able to handle any additional challenges, adversity, or stress. So, we potentially end up with insomnia, irritable bowel syndrome, constipation, reduced appetite, a weakened immune system, heart palpitations, and high blood pressure because all of our resources are going toward being primed and ready to fight or flee from the next threat of danger.

If we are stuck in a freeze response for a long time, we may experience depression, headaches and migraines, chronic fatigue, exhaustion, eating disorders, autoimmune issues, metabolic disease, and chronic pain.

As you can see, trauma and the symptoms of narcissistic abuse can leave a lasting imprint upon our health and well-being even beyond the (potential) ending of the narcissistic relationship. It's important to seek out the advice of a medical professional if you are experiencing any of the symptoms above; however, I hope you can understand with more clarity that while your body may have been adversely affected by the chronic trauma you have experienced, it has also been doing an incredible job of keeping you safe.

Gabor Maté, a world-renowned trauma specialist and physician, has done a lot of research on the impact of trauma on health and well-being. In his most recent book, *The Myth of Normal: Trauma, Illness, and Healing in a Toxic Culture*, Maté said, "Disease itself is both a culmination of what came before and a pointer to how things might unfold in the future. Our emotional dynamics, including our relationship to ourselves, can be among the powerful determinants of that future."[8] Therefore, improving your most important relationship, the one with yourself, is vital to unlocking greater well-being in the future.

---

8 Gabor Maté, *The Myth of Normal: Trauma, Illness, and Healing in a Toxic Culture* (Penguin Publishing Group, 2022), 90.

Part Four

Healing

Chapter Fourteen

Aftermath of a Narcissistic Relationship and Post-separation Abuse

Healing from narcissistic abuse doesn't happen the moment you end the relationship with the narcissist. It is a journey that involves awareness, understanding, validation, regulation, and self-discovery.

While it may feel like a weight has been lifted off your shoulders the moment you've ended the relationship with the narcissist, it doesn't mean the invisible wounds from the psychological, emotional, and verbal abuse have automatically disappeared. They still need tender, loving care and time to heal.

One of the first things I encourage you to do in the aftermath of a narcissistic relationship is to take as much time as you need for yourself so you can process, grieve, and recover. This is often called the cocoon phase or the fifth stage of the narcissistic abuse cycle.

We didn't discuss the cocoon phase in chapter three when we walked through the abuse cycle because it is not initiated by the narcissist. It is the final stage *after* the relationship ends. That does not mean it is any less important. As a matter of fact, it is the *most* important phase for your healing and recovery, as it is implemented and, hopefully, held sacred by you.

Know that you are worthy of taking all the time and space you need to pick up the pieces. There may be a part of you that still feels lost and confused and that's understandable; you've been through a lot. Another part of you may feel angry and bitter at the narcissist or even toward yourself for having not ended the relationship sooner. There may be days when you feel both immense joy and extreme sadness. All of it is okay and completely normal. Please don't ever make yourself wrong for feeling whatever it is you are feeling.

Many of my clients eventually get to a place where they beat themselves up for not having seen the red flags sooner. The thing is, you couldn't have known what you now know until you did. Meaning, you were operating at the level of awareness you had in the moment. You can't change that, no matter how much you wish you could, so stop beating yourself up for it. Hopefully, there are some positive things that came out of the relationship as well. Maybe it's children, maybe it's a stronger sense of who you are or what you want for your life, or maybe it's the strength, resilience, and courage you have uncovered as a result of the experience. There is always something to be grateful for, even if that feels hard at the moment. It will come.

Now, there may be a part of you that would like an apology, and you may have the hope that if you explain to the narcissist how you felt and what you experienced in the relationship, it may illicit the apology you're so desperate to hear.

I am sorry to say that if you continue to engage with the narcissist with an underlying motivation of receiving an apology, you will be sorely disappointed and may suffer unnecessary post-separation abuse that could be avoided if you're able to cut ties.

As previously mentioned, narcissists rarely take full accountability for their actions. Even if they apologize, pay close attention to their words because they will likely shift some of the responsibility onto you, someone else, or external circumstances. If it's not their words that betray them, it will be their actions.

For example, a narcissist may claim to take accountability for why the relationship has ended and even apologize for their actions. However, they might simultaneously drag out the divorce process or repeatedly question why the divorce is necessary. They may insist they do not understand why the relationship must end. This subtle tactic, often seen in covert narcissists, highlights how their actions and words frequently contradict each other.

Narcissists in general usually betray themselves. Their words and their actions tend not to align, so they may say one thing and do another. When they proffer empty apologies, you may be left feeling even more unheard, unseen, and misunderstood.

Seeking an apology from a narcissist or even expecting them to understand how much they've hurt you continues to place the power in their hands. Don't leave yourself vulnerable to their mistreatment and manipulation. More importantly, please don't give them the opportunity to disempower you further.

While most experts would encourage you to go "no contact" with the narcissist in order to begin healing, I understand that it may not be possible if you share children, work together, or are the adult child of an aging narcissistic parent. Having to remain in contact with the narcissist if you are unable to terminate the relationship can be tricky, and sadly, it leaves you vulnerable to post-separation abuse.

Post-separation abuse is a very real thing, whether you cut ties or not, so it's important to discuss it so you can be prepared.

Here are some of the abusive tactics a narcissist may use post-separation:

Flying Monkeys

Once you cut ties with a narcissist or reduce the contact you two have, the narcissist may potentially rope in people closest to you to continue the abuse. These people are called flying monkeys, similar to the those in the movie *The Wizard of Oz*.

These flying monkeys are manipulated by the narcissist who is likely feeding them lies and questionable narratives so that they act at the behest of the narcissist.

Often, the narcissist will play the wounded victim, building sympathy with the flying monkeys who only want to help. These flying monkeys will often also struggle with boundaries and, as a result, may insert themselves into your personal dealings with the narcissist or create more drama between you and the narcissist.

This could look like
- harassing you to find out why you can't forgive the narcissist or trying to get you two back together;

- unknowingly manipulating you for information that is shared with the narcissist behind your back and is later used against you (playing both sides);
- spreading and repeating the narcissist's lies about you to other people (perpetuating the abuse);
- siding with the narcissist and feeling bad for them, causing the person to maintain a friendship with the narcissist while cutting ties with you (which can be very hurtful if it's close family members or friends);
- advocating for the narcissist and how good of a person they are to make you feel guilty and ashamed for "letting them go," causing you to doubt your decision. (Flying monkeys will meddle and try to negotiate on behalf of the narcissist to get you to reignite the relationship.)

The ultimate goal of the narcissist with this tactic is to further isolate you from close family and friends by playing the victim, while portraying you as the crazy one, the villain, the persecutor, or the cheater. They may also have an ulterior motive of trying to win you back by using other people as pawns to bid your favor.

Smear Campaign

The narcissist will utilize flying monkeys to enact a smear campaign which involves discrediting, devaluing, and demeaning you to others in order to again destroy your reputation and further isolate you from the people closest to you. Since the narcissist can no longer hurt you, he or she will attempt to do this through other people. Of course, the narcissist may also attempt to do this via social media or by making public declarations that to damage your image, reputation, or close relationships.

Future Faking/Baiting

This is where the narcissist will share the *shoulda, woulda, couldas*, as I like to say, about how amazing the future could have been had you stayed with them. They will use every opportunity they can to continue to instill doubt in your mind that you made the right decision in letting them go. This may also happen in the hoovering phase. They will dangle the carrot or bait and hope you bite. If you don't take the bait, they will make pointed comments about all the amazing things they plan to do now that the relationship is over—often things you wanted to do while you were still with them. This is their way of reminding you that now that you aren't together, you can't do them anymore, and it's your loss. Don't take the bait! This future faking and baiting often includes claims that they are changing or *will* change, becoming a better person, and suggesting that if only you had given them another chance, your family could still "be whole." (Sidenote: Your family isn't broken because of the divorce—it's simply been beautifully reorganized!) If you hear this or something similar, run. They are manipulating you into feeling guilty or afraid that you are missing out, with the hope that you'll be inspired to turn around and run back into their arms. Do not. These are just more strings in the web of lies they wish to ensnare you in once again.

Legal and Financial Abuse

They may file frivolous lawsuit after frivolous lawsuit as a means of harassing you. They may also make false claims or allegations or drag out divorce or custody proceedings just to make your life miserable. They may project and claim that you were the abusive one or the one with a drug problem, for example. Stay strong, stand firm. Use grounding techniques and somatic tools to manage your emotions and be sure to have a strong network of friends, loved ones, and of course professionals who can support you. Do not allow yourself to be taken advantage of.

Stalking/Monitoring

The narcissist may go to extreme measures to keep tabs on you wherever you are as a way to intimidate you and maintain control. It would not be beneath them to cyberstalk you or use a third party to gather information to use against you. I've heard awful stories of narcissistic exes planting AirTags in children's backpacks so they can track where they are when they are with the other parent or installing tracking devices in exes' cars (which were hard for even the police to find) or using social media to track someone's whereabouts using fake profiles. If you feel unsafe, contact the authorities or an attorney.

Manipulating Children/Parental Alienation

Using your children as pawns is not beneath the narcissist if it helps them maintain control. They may contact the children during your time with them, asking questions to gather information about your whereabouts and whom you are with. They may say disparaging things about you to the kids in an attempt to poison them against you. They may manipulate the kids into divulging private and personal information about you or involve the children in adult matters. They may also say or do things to put the kids in awkward situations where they feel they have to choose one parent over the other. This not only damages you but also, and more importantly, deeply hurts the children. No child should ever be alienated from a parent, even if you and their co-parent have a toxic relationship. The only time a child should be kept from one of their caregivers is if the environment is violent or dangerous or if there is physical endangerment. If you suspect your narcissistic ex is trying to poison your children against you, please seek the support of a qualified therapist for your children and also for you, because it can be very difficult to navigate.

Withholding Support

The narcissist may refuse to provide financial/child support or make receiving support as difficult as possible. Again, this is to keep them in control and to cause you aggravation. If you are upset or angry, then that means they still have influence and control over you.

Emotional and Psychological Manipulation

Just because the relationship is over does not mean the narcissist will stop using emotional and psychological manipulation tactics such as gaslighting, emotional blackmail, or threats. They may harass you via text, email, in person, or over the phone. They will do all they can to continue to undermine your sense of reality, whittle away your self-worth, and cause you to doubt your decision.

When co-parenting with a narcissistic ex, it's important to have extremely modified contact. This means that you *only* communicate on an as-needed basis. This may feel difficult to do if you're used to texting your ex; however, all that texting back and forth keeps you vulnerable to more post-separation abuse, which may leave you feeling overwhelmed and dysregulated rather than calm, cool, and collected.

Here are some suggestions:
1. Move all communication to written form so you have a track record in the event it is needed for legal proceedings. That means no phone calls. Use only email or text. If you opt for text, see number two below.
2. Create an email address and a Google Voice number specifically for your ex. Tell your ex you got a new number and created a new email address just for them so their messages do not get lost among everything else because you want to prioritize their messages, especially for when it comes to communicating about the kids. Then block your ex's phone number and email address on your phone and your email provider.
3. You will then need to set internal boundaries around how often you check your Google Voice text messages and your new email address. Perhaps you check it once a day, using a somatic tool before and after to feel grounded and calm. If the children are with your ex, you may wish to check it more frequently, especially if your child or children are not old enough to have their own phones or devices. The best part about Google Voice is that it will require anyone calling to state their name before you accept the call. Therefore, you will be less likely to be caught unaware that it is your ex (in case they get sneaky with trying to contact you from different numbers).
4. The other boundary you will need to set is around giving yourself time and space to downregulate and get back into a calm state before responding to any messages. If you find that your response is still too emotional, then you may want to run it through ChatGPT or run it by a friend who can help you tone it down and only share what is pertinent. Remove all emotion from any responses. Remember, if you show any kind of emotion, the narcissist will believe they still maintain some kind of control over you.

5. You may want to do handoffs at the end of your driveway or on the sidewalk to prevent your ex from entering your property, home, or apartment. Similarly, you will want to do the same if you are dropping off the kids at your ex's house. If your kids are old enough to enter your house on their own, then you will want to make sure they understand clearly that your ex is not to enter your home when you are not there, and they are not to share their key or access code to enter your home with your ex.
6. It's important to also block your ex on all social media accounts and avoid cyberstalking them to see what they are up to, whom they may be dating, etc. It's not worth your emotional energy. This may also involve setting clear boundaries with any mutual friends or family members who may feel compelled to share what your ex is up without your asking. Let them know you'd prefer not to discuss your ex's personal life or hear any gossip pertaining to them.

Now it is time to focus on your own healing and recovery! Hopefully, up to this point, this book has brought awareness of the patterns, traits, and behaviors of a narcissist as well as your own. I hope it has also helped you understand the abuse cycle, why it can feel very difficult to break the trauma bond that it creates, and how you ended up in such a toxic relationship. Furthermore, I hope it provided you with some validation of your experience of narcissistic abuse.

If you have decided to remain in the narcissistic relationship, no judgment; however, I want to caution you against something that may have crossed your mind: couples counseling. I mentioned this in a previous chapter however, it bears repeating:

Please, please, please, I implore you not to attempt couples counseling with a narcissist.

First, it is possible that the sessions may escalate the abuse with the narcissist getting angry about you blowing their perfectly curated self-image to the therapist. As a result, they may gaslight you further, enter into more rageful fits, or possibly even begin to physically abuse you as they become more desperate to control you.

A therapy room with a narcissist is not a safe space because of the repercussions that follow.

Second, the narcissist is likely going to gaslight and manipulate the therapist. While there are some very good therapists out there who would be able to identify the narcissist a mile away, there are plenty of others who would not see through their antics. They may believe the narcissist's charming, good-guy persona and not really understand what's happening behind closed doors. Instead, I suggest you each get your own individual therapist and focus on your own inner work.

Third, as we discussed, the narcissist is never really going to change, no matter how motivated they appear to be in the short-term. In the long run, they will revert right back to their old, toxic, abusive coping mechanisms and defense patterns because they lack the self-awareness that what they are doing is harmful. They are too afraid to look themselves in the mirror and see who they are, because they are so deeply wounded and insecure that it's scary to be that vulnerable. They have adapted these manipulative behaviors as a way to stay safe, and the behaviors have worked up until this point, so the narcissist has little reason to change. They believe they are a good person and likely that *you* are the problem, not them.

Therefore, it is so important that instead of focusing on fixing the relationship or changing the narcissist, or even on the toxic past you two shared, focus only on what you *can* change going forward, and that is you!

The next part of the journey is about healing and recovery. It involves learning how to regulate your nervous system after spending years in fight or flight, learning to set boundaries (boundaries are so underrated!), and rediscovering the true essence of who you are. This all takes time, and the process of both healing and recovery can be beautiful, provided you give yourself the compassion, time, space, and grace to allow your healing and recovery to unfold.

You can only move as quickly as your nervous system will allow to avoid further shutdown or getting stuck in survival mode.

After getting out of a narcissistic relationship, you may feel like you've lost your purpose or that you've lost yourself completely. The trauma you have experienced has likely disconnected you from your innate power, your ability to trust yourself (and others), and the memory of just how truly brilliant you are. Your self-worth, confidence, and courage may have been chiseled away. I often say narcissistic abuse is like experiencing death by a thousand papers cuts.

The good news is that you are not broken, even if you've been made to feel that way. There is nothing wrong with you. Healing and recovering from narcissistic abuse are absolutely possible, and guess what? As the saying goes, "The comeback is greater than the setback."

My hope for you is to see that in order to get to know who you truly are, you had to first get to know who you are not. The narcissist helped you see, ultimately, who you are not so you could get clear on who you actually are, what you want, and who you aspire to become.

My hope is that one day, you get to a place in your healing where you are able to look at the narcissist with compassion. While you may not ever forgive them, I hope you are able to at least be grateful for the lessons you have learned that have brought you into closer alignment with who you truly are. I hope you are able to transform the pain of the past into the most authentic and empowered version of who you are.

Chapter Fifteen

THE KEY TO HEALING

Nervous system regulation is essential to healing from trauma. Full stop.

After spending years in a dysregulated state, walking on eggshells, feeling constantly on edge, waiting for the next shoe to drop, or feeling like a zombie in your own apocalyptic world, it is *imperative* to work with your nervous system to feel safe, calm, and grounded.

If you ended up in a narcissistic relationship, there is likely a chance you were chasing love, attention, and safety outside of yourself. In the aftermath, you may come to realize that everything you need—love, attention, and safety—are all within you.

First things first: We need to create safety within so you can radiate out all the love you have on those who deserve it.

To work effectively with your nervous system, it's essential to first recognize when you're triggered into one of the four trauma responses: fight, flight, freeze, or fawn.

The nervous system, according to Dr. Stephen Porges's polyvagal theory moves in a hierarchical order through three different states in response to varying levels of stress and perceived threats. Those three distinct states are the ventral vagal state (social engagement system and calm), the sympathetic state (fight or flight), and the dorsal vagal state (shutdown and freeze).

Below is an illustration of the various nervous system states:

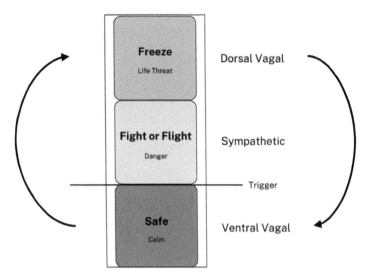

We move from ventral vagal to sympathetic once we are triggered or detect danger or a threat. If the threat or danger persists, we move into dorsal vagal. In order to come back down to ventral vagal, feeling safe, we need to move down through the sympathetic state. Adapted from the work of Stephen W. Porges.[9]

Let's discuss each nervous system state in more detail.

When you are feeling safe and grounded, you are in what we call a ventral vagal state. It is also known as the social engagement system, and it is where we feel present, calm, focused, ready to connect with others, and capable of handling the challenges life brings.

Neuroception is the autonomic nervous system's way of subconsciously scanning and responding to internal and external cues of risk or danger. It is below our level of awareness, which is why we may get triggered by a change in environment, someone's facial expression, a critical remark, or a gesture.

As part of the function of neuroception, our nervous system reacts to what it perceives to be a threat. After experiencing chronic trauma or stress, your body may perceive a threat even when there is none. This is called a neuroceptive mismatch. For example, if you are primed to be hypervigilant due to trauma, it is possible that

---

[9] Stephen W. Porges, *The Pocket Guide to the Polyvagal Theory: The Transformative Power of Feeling Safe* (W.W. Norton & Company, 2011).

even a sudden loud noise, like a book crashing to the ground, might send you into a prolonged activation of the fight or flight response. This heightened startle reflex, where your nervous system is unable to calm itself down even after the "threat" has passed, is an example of a neuroceptive mismatch.

When you are triggered, pay attention to the sensations you are feeling in your body. As I mentioned, the nervous system moves through a hierarchy so when we are first triggered, we move into a sympathetic nervous system state or a fight or flight response.

In a fight or flight response, you may notice an increase in your breathing or heart rate, or you may feel jittery, nauseous, anxious, or sweaty. The sensations come first and serve as your initial clue that you've been triggered. Next will be the emotions, thoughts, beliefs, and potentially images or memories of past relational trauma.

Some of the emotions that arise in a sympathetic state might be anger, worry, frustration, and fear.

If the risk or threat persists or escalates, your nervous system will move into a dorsal vagal state, or a freeze or fawn response. Some of the sensations you might experience in this state are a slowed heart rate, even slower breathing, shaking, trembling, or feeling cold. The emotions that may be felt in a dorsal vagal state are grief, depression, confusion, devastation, or shock. Or you may feel completely shut down, numb, exhausted, or dissociated from any feelings or sensations. There are neurobiological processes at play when this happens, as the body is preparing for what it anticipates will be excruciatingly painful, possibly even death. As a result, it releases opioids to numb the body from any potential sensations of life-threatening pain. As an example, in the animal kingdom, an animal that perceives an escalated threat to their survival might play dead.

Understanding your triggers and the core wounds being poked and prodded in those moments will bring you even greater awareness and provide deeper insights into what is happening on a subconscious level. This will allow you to address the root cause of your reactions.

A core wound is a deep emotional injury or trauma, often rooted in limiting beliefs formed during your early childhood, typically before you were verbal, and later reinforced through life experiences. According to Dr. Bruce Lipton, most of our subconscious programming was formed between birth and two years old. These core wounds are reflected in the subconscious beliefs we hold about ourselves and often stem from dysfunctional family dynamics, attachment wounds, or childhood trauma.

We spend 90 to 99 percent of our day operating from our subconscious programming, according to Dr. Bruce Lipton in his book *The Biology of Belief*. If that programming is filled with negative beliefs, then we are likely making decisions, behaving, or acting not from a true sense of self but rather a negative, fearful, hurt self.

Children before the age of nine years old live in a very me-centric world. Therefore, when things happen around them, good or bad, they tend to believe they are to blame. For a child who grows up in a dysfunctional family or where abuse is present, this can have a detrimental impact.

When there is not enough information about why something happened or whose fault it was, children tend to fill in the gaps with stories about themselves and what that experience means about them. This narrative may be positive or negative, depending on their limited perception.

Think about what a child is learning between the ages of birth and two years old. They undergo a rapid transformation as they learn to crawl, walk, run, talk, and feed themselves. If every time the child does something, the parent corrects the child by saying, "No, no, no. That's not safe!" or "No, no, no, that's not how we do/say that. We do/say it this way," the child learns that nothing they do is right.

This method of corrective parenting can be internalized by the young child as an internal belief or core wound that they aren't good enough. This idea of not being enough is ultimately, in my opinion, at the core of most core wounds and self-limiting beliefs. For example, they may think the following:

> *I am not lovable—because I am not enough.*
> *I am not worthy—because I am not enough.*
> *I am not valuable—because I don't DO enough.*

I am not important—because I don't (insert XYZ, i.e., know, have, achieve, love, etc.) enough.

These are just several of the typical core wounds. Others might include thinking the following:

I don't belong—because I am not enough (too different, not lovable, unlikable).

I am not special—because I am not (insert XYZ, i.e., smart, skinny, pretty, successful, athletic, talented, etc.) enough.

Once these core beliefs or wounds become instilled, we tend to carry them subconsciously throughout our adult lives. Some carry these beliefs until the day they die. Others, like you, dig deep to uncover them and work hard to reprogram them into something more affirmative and to stop allowing them to dictate actions, behaviors, and thoughts.

These core wounds and rewriting these limiting beliefs can be difficult, but once you are able to identify and become aware of which belief or wound may be triggered, you are able to then use somatic tools to downregulate and respond in a more emotionally regulated and thoughtful way.

It is not always easy to do, but with patience, self-compassion, and practice, you'll be able to increase the flexibility in your nervous system so that you can increase the gap between being triggered and your response. Knowing what you need in order to downregulate and get back to feeling safe and grounded before responding in a heated moment can have a meaningful impact on all of your relationships, whether that is with loved ones, friends, coworkers, or a narcissistic ex.

While it is important to be aware of triggers, I'd also love to invite you to become aware of your glimmers as well. Glimmers are the things that help you feel connected, grounded, curious, and ready to connect with others. For example, that may be dancing, listening to your favorite upbeat playlist, or going to dinner with friends. Knowing what helps you to either move back or stay in a ventral vagal state is equally important.

As you identify your triggers and glimmers, recognize which somatic tools, shared in chapter nine and explained further in chapter seventeen, help you to move between the various nervous system states.

Doing this work is just a part of the self-discovery process, and it is necessary if you want to be able to remain in the driver's seat as your true Self, rather than the emotional, inner child who is feeling hurt, scared, or threatened. This is a lot of the work I do in my coaching practice and that I train others to be able to do with their clients.

Oftentimes, those who have experienced narcissistic abuse have been told that they need to set and maintain clearer and more firm boundaries if they want to create healthier relationships. The problem is that those who end up in narcissistic relationships often have never been good at setting boundaries, which is partly why they ended up with the narcissist to begin with, and part of the reason is that having their boundaries tested triggered a fawn response. Or their nervous system shut down or engaged in people pleasing as a coping mechanism before they were even able to set a boundary. They may not have felt safe to set the boundary to begin with, or alternatively, they did not feel safe enforcing it.

On the other hand, anyone who has ever set a boundary with a narcissist knows that even if you set a boundary, they will most often ignore, dismiss, or violate the boundary anyway. The key is to set internal boundaries (more on that in chapter nineteen).

The name of the game is to go slowly. You can only move at the pace your nervous system will allow. Bringing somatic tools (refer back to the QR code shared in chapter nine for my top somatic tools) into a daily practice will help you increase the flexibility in your nervous system, but also, don't try to set a vulnerable or complicated boundary your first go around. Simply start by finding the power and courage to say no to something you don't want to do, without explaining the reason. As you demonstrate to your doubting mind that you *are* capable of setting boundaries, it will become easier as you continue to build the evidence of your ability to keep yourself safe.

The added benefit of setting boundaries is the gradual rebuilding of self-trust, which is often eroded after experiencing a narcissistic relationship. Each time you set a boundary and honor it by working with your nervous system to navigate any discomfort that may arise, you reinforce your ability to keep yourself safe. As you continue to create safety within, your sense of self-trust will grow and blossom. This process not only reinforces your ability to protect yourself but also nurtures a deep inner confidence that you can rely on yourself. Over time, this newfound self-trust becomes a powerful foundation for your healing and empowers you to navigate relationships with clarity and resilience. The next time red flags arise, you'll trust yourself to recognize and act on them!

Chapter Sixteen

PICKING UP THE PIECES: REDISCOVERING WHO YOU ARE

After enduring years of narcissistic abuse, many feel as though they have lost their sense of self. They often lament that they no longer recognize the person staring back at them in the mirror. Those who were once optimistic and adventurous find themselves resentful, pessimistic, and withdrawn. Others who were once the life of the party have become reclusive and antisocial. This is typical and not unusual. You have been conditioned by the narcissist to not shine too bright or be too energetic, successful, or happy because then the narcissist would engage in a devaluation campaign. You may not have been consciously aware it was happening, but you learned, nevertheless, to temper your personality, accomplishments, etc., and to disconnect from your Self.

Wouldn't it be nice to have a road map that could point you back in the direction of your lost sense of Self or, even better, understand the reasons you ended up in a toxic relationship?

Well, let me reintroduce you to Human Design, which we discussed a bit in chapter eight. Human Design is a synthesis of five ancient wisdoms: the Jewish Kabbalah, Hindu chakra system, Chinese *I Ching*, Eastern and Western astrology, and quantum physics.

The beauty of the system lies in its simplicity and objectivity in its assessment. Unlike qualitative personality tests, which can be easily influenced by your current mood, experiences, or how you see yourself today versus in the past or future, this system relies solely on your birth date, time, and place. It's that straightforward!

Now, it's important to note that Human Design is not meant to define or label you in any kind of way. Nor does it tell you how you should be living your life or where you went wrong. Rather, it shows you all of your potential in varying degrees from high to low expressions. Up until this point, you have unconsciously decided how to express and embody your unique energetic blueprint. Once you begin to peel back the layers of your Human Design and get to know it more intimately, you can then begin to experiment with how you wish to express the potentials available to you, which are endless.

There are some lower expressions of the chart that can explain why you may have leaned into codependent tendencies, which are beyond the scope of this discussion. However, I always find it interesting when I notice them during my discussions with clients, as the Human Design chart is a tool I refer to in my coaching practice.

While there are many layers and aspects of the Human Design chart that can be helpful when trying to reconnect back to your true Self, it can also guide you toward learning how to trust yourself again. It can show you how to open up to the deep wisdom that's already inside of you and how to access your clarity when making big decisions.

This is crucial after experiencing narcissistic abuse, since you have likely disconnected from your intuition and/or stopped trusting your ability to make good decisions for yourself.

I am going to attempt to briefly teach you how you are meant to make big decisions that are aligned for you according to your Human Design chart since you may be at a turning point in your life where you are facing a lot of them. Even if you are not, this will help you, regardless. It will also help you begin to trust that you *are* capable of making good and healthy decisions for yourself.

First things first, if you do have not already have a copy of your Human Design chart, then scan this QR code below with your phone and input your information so you can download your free copy:

If you have no clue how to scan a QR code with your phone's camera, here is the link: https://bit.ly/runyourhdchart.

The part of the chart we will focus on, which reveals how you are designed to make major life decisions in your life, is your Strategy and Authority. While your Strategy is dependent upon your Type, we will not be diving too deeply into your Type. I'll provide you with another resource shortly where you can learn more about your Type.

For now, look on the left-hand side of the chart you just ran and identify your Type, Strategy, and Authority. It will be denoted toward the top of the report.

Your Strategy informs how you are meant to interact with the world around you so that you can tap into the universal flow of energy and attract new opportunities, experiences, and relationships into your life with ease.

Your Authority is how you are meant to make aligned decisions that are right for you. Your Type, in case you were wondering, describes how you are meant to optimally use your energy in the world so that you do not deplete or drain your internal resources.

While I'd love to teach you how to understand all of the nuances of your chart, I recognize it might also feel overwhelming at this stage. It is therefore my intention to merely introduce this tool to you in a way that highlights the key aspects that would be most helpful.

According to Human Design, each individual has a distinct method for making decisions, guided by their Strategy, which is based on their Type and further shaped by their Authority. Your Authority is how your intuition is meant to make decisions in the moment.

Let's first break down Type and Strategy:

Type: Manifestor
Strategy: Needs to inform others before taking action

A Manifestor is here to initiate and follow their sparks of inspiration; however, they need to inform others before they take action because sometimes their fast-moving energy can be overwhelming to others. By informing, they settle the energy field around them.

Type: Generator
Strategy: Needs to wait to respond

A Generator is not here to initiate but rather to respond to the opportunities, experiences, and people around them. They have the energy to pursue opportunities and get things done, but they need to do it in alignment with their Strategy and Authority.

Type: Manifesting Generator
Strategy: Needs to inform before taking action and wait to respond

A Manifesting Generator is a mix of a Manifestor and a Generator. They can have a lot of energy and may often juggle many balls in the air at one time. They are multi-passionate. However, they need to inform others before they take action and wait to respond first. They are not here to initiate like the Manifestor.

Type: Projector
Strategy: Needs to wait for the invitation or recognition

A Projector is here to guide others to fulfill their greatest potential, which they can clearly see. They need to wait to be recognized by others before sharing their guidance or for the invitation to share so that their guidance is well received.

Type: Reflector
Strategy: Needs to wait a full Lunar cycle (28 days)

A Reflector is a very wise observer who amplifies and reflects to others what they observe. Observing others takes time and so it is important they are surrounded by the right people in order to become aligned. As such, they need to wait a full Lunar cycle before making any big decisions. They do not have their own Authority. Their Strategy informs how they are meant to make big decisions.

Now let's dive into Authority. There are five different types of Authority: Splenic, Sacral, Ego-manifested, Emotional, and Self-projected or Mental Authority. Locate which one you have according to your chart and then read the details on the corresponding Authority below.

Splenic Authority

If you have Splenic Authority, you are meant to make decisions that align with your intuition. Your intuition will come through as a quiet, soft-spoken knowing. It is unemotional and free of fear and doesn't make demands. This subtle intuitive hit can be challenging to discern from fear, as fear tends to be louder and more emotional and is often accompanied by a narrative or internal dialogue.

For Generators with a Splenic Authority, the strong response of your Sacral Authority, which we will cover next, will likely drown out your intuitive Splenic pulse, particularly when making significant decisions. Additionally, if a trauma or core wound is triggered, you may experience a fear response rather than an intuitive hit, making it even more difficult to discern.

To make decisions aligned with your Splenic Authority, it's essential to slow things down and create quiet moments so you can hear your intuition. Your intuition may communicate with you in multiple ways or in one specific way. You may hear it as a quiet voice, feel certain sensations, receive messages in dreams or visions, or even experience a sense of smell or taste that signals what feels right or wrong.

Learning to recognize how your intuition speaks to you is key. The best way to develop this awareness is by slowing down, spending time in silence, and observing how these signals arise in your life. This practice will help you trust your Splenic guidance when faced with big decisions.

Sacral Authority

If you have Sacral Authority, your decision-making process will be guided by an immediate gut-level response. This gut instinct is often accompanied by specific sounds and sensations. The Sacral typically responds with sounds like "uh-huh" and "unh-unh" or "um-hmm" and "unn-uhm," which indicate affirmative or negative reactions.

If you struggle to connect with your sacral sounds, you're not alone. Many with the Sacral Authority have been disconnected from these natural responses early in life, as parents often discouraged grunting or nonverbal sounds and encouraged verbal answers instead. Reconnecting your sacral motor will take practice, but it's entirely possible.

One way to retrain your sacral is by asking yourself yes or no questions. For example, stand in front of your fridge and ask, "Do I want fruit?" Try to answer the question with sacral sounds rather than using words. If your sacral responds with a "unh-unh" or "unn-uhm," then ask, "Do I want a yogurt?" Keep going until you get an affirmative sacral response. If your mind interferes, focus on the physical sensations in your body instead.

A "hell yes" from your sacral may feel expansive, like a rush of energy, a buzzing (not butterflies!) in your gut, or a pull forward. A "hell no" will feel more like a contraction, a lack of energy, or a pull inward. To refine your clarity, it can also be helpful to have someone ask you yes or no questions, allowing you to tune in to your immediate, authentic response. By practicing and observing these cues, you'll strengthen your connection to your Sacral Authority and make more aligned decisions.

Sidenote: If you are a Manifesting Generator with the 34-20 channel defined (a red, black, or both colored line from the number 20 to the number 34 on the chart), then whatever sound comes out of your mouth first is your sacral sound. It may be "yes," "yup," "yeah," "okay," "no," "nope," "nah," or any other variation, including short phrases.

Ego-manifested Authority

If you have Ego-manifested Authority, it's essential to first ensure you have the energy and are well-rested enough to take action on the decision. Next, pay attention to the cues and clues from the Universe that indicate right timing. These might come in the form of synchronicities, signs, conversations, or messages.

Talking through things can also be beneficial, as it helps you gain clarity about right timing and assess whether you have the necessary resources—whether energetic, financial, skills, or time—to move forward confidently.

Emotional Authority

If you have Emotional Authority, it's important to give yourself time to gain clarity. Sleeping on a decision or waiting a few days while regularly checking in with yourself is often the best approach. During these check-ins, if you notice you more often feel unenthusiastic about an opportunity, it's likely not the right time or the right opportunity to pursue. On the other hand, if you more frequently feel excited about the idea or opportunity over several days, it's likely a sign that the timing and the opportunity are right.

Allowing yourself to wait out your emotional highs and lows is important when you have Emotional Authority. Observing whether your moods follow a pattern can also provide valuable insights during the decision-making process.

Self-projected/Mental Authority

If you have Self-projected or Mental Authority, your clarity comes through talking things out with others. To make aligned decisions, it's important to find someone who can serve as a neutral sounding board, someone who will listen without offering advice, suggestions, guidance, or judgment. Speaking your thoughts aloud to this kind of supportive listener allows you to hear yourself more clearly and make the decision that feels most aligned with your authentic self.

I hope the above helps you understand how opportunities are meant to come your way (through your Strategy) and how you are meant to decide whether the timing is right and if the opportunities are aligned (through your Authority) for you.

There is just one other aspect of the Human Design chart that I would like to address. Pull out your chart and observe the triangle on the right-hand side, toward the bottom. We call this triangle your Emotional Solar Plexus, and it's responsible for processing your emotional energy. Let's discuss in more detail how your emotional energy works.

If your Emotional Solar Plexus is undefined, or white, in the chart, then you may identify as an empath. As an empath, you have a natural tendency to absorb and amplify the emotional energy of those around you. This is especially important to understand if you are a codependent empath, as codependents often tend to take responsibility for other people's emotions. The combination of absorbing, amplifying, and taking responsibility for other people's emotions can be overwhelming and draining. For this reason, it is vital to learn how to discern the difference between your emotions and those of others.

Staying grounded in your discernment is crucial when navigating emotional energy. With an undefined Emotional Solar Plexus, you may also notice a tendency to avoid speaking your truth to sidestep confrontation. Does this pattern sound familiar as a codependent trait? In response to the discomfort of others' strong or negative emotions, you may have learned to shut down your feelings to stay safe, which aligns with the freeze response (dorsal vagal). Alternatively, you may have turned to people pleasing as a way to manage the discomfort of absorbing and amplifying other people's emotional energy, a behavior often tied to the fawn response (dorsal vagal). For example, if those around you were happy, you could feel happy too, as a way of maintaining the harmony.

While other parts of the chart may also indicate tendencies toward being an empath or people pleaser, this explanation focuses specifically on the role of an undefined Emotional Solar Plexus. Understanding this aspect of your design can help you create healthier emotional boundaries and foster greater self-awareness.

If your Emotional Solar Plexus is defined, or colored in, on the chart, you experience emotional energy as a wave. There are various types of emotional waves, which we will not address here, but it is essential to understand that experiencing emotional highs and lows is completely normal for you. Tracking your moods over a thirty-day period can help you observe patterns in your wave and better understand how it fluctuates.

It's recommended that you avoid making any decisions during the high or low points of your wave. Instead, aim to decide when your emotions feel steady and balanced. Nervous system regulation can be an invaluable tool in helping you achieve this steadiness. However, it's important to note that regulating your emotions does not mean suppressing them—you must still allow yourself to feel your emotions and give them the space they need to be processed.

It's also important to understand how your emotions might impact your loved ones, particularly your children. If their Emotional Solar Plexuses are undefined, your children may absorb and amplify your emotional wave, experiencing highs and lows more intensely. By regulating your emotions, you not only support your own well-being but also help your children learn to regulate their emotions more effectively. This awareness and self-regulation can create a more harmonious environment for everyone.

This is why I absolutely love Human Design! It offers profound insights into ourselves and our loved ones in practical and meaningful ways. When combined with what you've learned about nervous system regulation, attachment styles, family dynamics, and codependency, it can supercharge your growth and personal expansion!

If you'd like to dive deeper into your Human Design Type, Strategy, Authority, and Profile Lines, I invited you to check out my free HD 101 course. You can access it at your convenience using the QR code below:

Or use this link: https://bit.ly/HD101.

Alternatively, I encourage you to check out two of my mentors, Karen Curry Parker and Emma Dunwoody. Both have resources, courses, and books on Human Design that can help you utilize and understand the system in a very practical way.

Human Design is a rich and complex system, but to keep it simple and avoid overwhelm, focusing on how you are designed to make aligned decisions and how your emotional energy works are is the most impactful way to start when recovering from narcissistic abuse. I encourage you to watch the video in the HD 101 course about your Energy Type and, if you're curious, explore the ones on your Profile Lines as well. The more you understand about yourself, the better equipped you'll be to create a life aligned with your true nature.

The Human Design chart includes many layers: 64 gates, 9 energy centers, 32 channels, and 13 planetary positions (x2 for conscious and unconscious aspects). Your chart is uniquely expressed through the interaction of these elements, influenced by both your definition (colored-in areas) and openness (white areas), as well as your life experiences.

Ultimately, *you* bring your chart to life. This information is shared to inspire curiosity and invite you into a deeper exploration of who you are and how you express your unique potential. Think of it as a starting point for self-discovery—a journey that will continue to unfold throughout your life.

After having endured narcissistic trauma, you may feel disconnected from your sense of self. Human Design can be an invaluable tool to finding your way back to who *you* truly are, especially if you've been questioning who you are (identity) and why you're here (purpose). (Hint: Your purpose is to *be you* or your *Self!*)

By understanding the beautiful road map that Human Design provides, you can reconnect to your core self and help you begin trusting yourself again. It offers the pathway to reclaim your power, authenticity, and sovereignty. While that may seem like a lofty promise, I speak from personal experience and from witnessing how it has transformed the lives of countless clients.

Knowing who you are keeps you empowered and protects you from others who may try to control your narrative in the future. With a strong sense of self, you can rebuild your self-confidence and courage. If you're feeling disconnected from
your true self right now, rediscovering who you are can feel like coming home. It allows you to love yourself in a whole new, healthier way—a love that stops you from settling for anything less than you deserve.

Take this as an invitation, something to respond to, or a cue from the Universe, if it feels aligned for you. Should you wish to have your Human Design chart read, please feel free to reach out. I would be honored to share the brilliance of who you are through the lens of your chart.

Chapter Seventeen

REPARENTING THE INNER CHILD

In chapters eleven and twelve, we spoke about family dynamics and attachment wounds. Therefore, I would be remiss not to mention how part of the healing process involves healing our inner child.

Learning how to reparent ourselves is necessary so we can heal our past trauma and provide our inner child with all the love, reassurance, safety, and respect we may not have received as children.

When we experience trauma, the event itself may not be something we are able to recall. The pain, story, or limiting beliefs (a.k.a. wounds) we adapted in the aftermath do not get time-stamped into the past. As a result, our subconscious mind may actively recall the spiritual, emotional, or intellectual pain we may have experienced as if it is still happening in the present moment when we are triggered.

Being able to rewire the neural pathways around the limiting beliefs and stories we have adapted as a way to persevere and survive is absolutely possible, and finding the right support to do this internal work is essential.

There is a plethora of modalities you can utilize in order to do this subconscious reprogramming. Personally, I have tried many, and while I will share with you what has worked for me, please know that I encourage you to get curious and explore what modalities work best for you.

I prefer to use either Subconscious Belief Reprogramming™ or Emotional Freedom Technique. Subconscious Belief Reprogramming™ utilizes an inner-child meditation to help you, the adult, give the inner child what they needed and didn't receive as a child, helping to squash any limiting beliefs or stories that may have been adapted during specific time periods.

In EFT, or Emotional Freedom Technique, otherwise known as tapping, you tap on nine different meridian points in a specific sequence (as depicted below) to help you first enter into a ventral vagal state and then release the emotions or stagnant energy in the body related to a limiting belief, narrative, past trauma, or memory.

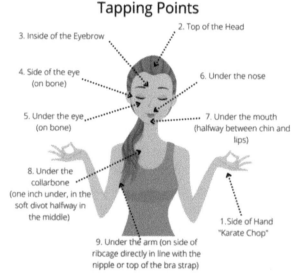

Both of these methods can be effective without having to recall or relive the past trauma or memory.

When we experience trauma, we often experience a whirlwind of emotions. If we internalize the experience and assign it a personal meaning—especially one that feels too painful to bear—we may develop unhealthy coping mechanisms to help us *avoid* confronting that deep pain or those overwhelming emotions.

Emotions are meant to be "energy (e) IN motion." When we don't allow ourselves to fully process and feel those emotions, they can become trapped within the body. EFT helps us release those stagnancies, and when we do, we can often see things from a different perspective. It enables us to rewrite or "tap in" a new, more affirmative belief or story. There is a lot more science behind it, and if you're interested in learning more about the science behind tapping, I encourage you to look up the research of Dr. Peta Stapleton.

In my coaching practice, I also incorporate Dr. Richard C. Schwartz's Internal Family Systems (IFS) theory.[10] Through IFS, we are able to understand the idea that different "parts" of us have come together to form, and protect, the Self. These protector parts consist of managers and firefighters, and their primary function is to help keep our exiles or inner-child wounds from being felt, experienced, or witnessed.

When we have experienced a lot of trauma over many years, these protector parts will show up on a daily basis. Over time, we may begin to self-identify with the parts that regularly show up to keep us safe. The healing comes when we learn how to "unblend" from our parts and stop them from running our lives.

When we approach these parts with curiosity and compassion and courageously explore why they are showing up, what they are protecting us from, and what they fear might happen if they stop doing their job, we open the door for our true, adult Self to take the lead.

When we look at this from an inner-child perspective, we begin to understand that certain protector parts may have been created at various points throughout our childhood as a way to keep us safe and to self-preserve. Other parts may have surfaced later through our life experiences. When we can identify the deep inner wound that the part is protecting us from (which exile), we are able to acknowledge, accept, and show gratitude for the job it has done to keep us safe up until this point.

When we integrate the nervous system into this equation, moments of distress or being triggered become opportunities for healing. By using an effective somatic tool to downregulate the nervous system, we can shift into a ventral vagal state, a place, as you recall, of safety, connection, and calm. From this state, we can approach the part of us that has been activated with curiosity and compassion.

---

10 Richard C. Schwartz, *Introduction to Internal Family Systems Model* (Trailheads Publishing, 2001).

We might begin by exploring the sensations, emotions, images, beliefs, or memories that arose when the part appeared. Often, these parts are coping strategies, distraction techniques, defense mechanisms, or avoidance tactics developed to protect us during stress of trauma. When we create safety within us by regulating our nervous system and allowing our emotions to move through us, we create space between the trigger and our response.

This space is key; it slows things down, allowing us to observe and understand these parts rather than acting impulsively. By combining somatic tools with self-awareness, we cultivate deeper connection with these protector parts, offering them the reassurance they need and enabling our true Self to take the lead with clarity and intention.

This is life-changing for you and your nearest and dearest. It can change the trajectory of your relationships. It can help you regain control over your life and reclaim your true, authentic Self.

When you're able to return to the present moment and feel safe enough to pause and then respond instead of being reactive, then the part may no longer need to jump into the driver's seat to keep you safe. Instead, the Self is able to more adeptly drive the bus, so to speak, forcing the protector part to take a backseat.

It's important to remember that there are no *bad* parts of you, only parts that are trying to do their absolute best to protect you and keep you safe. Your emotions are cues that your exiles (core wounds) have triggered. Some emotions are also parts, so it's important to feel your feelings and pay attention to what they are trying to share with you. They are often messengers that something is off. It may be that an unspoken boundary has been violated or a core wound was provoked.

When you feel anxiety, worry, anger, or frustration, there's a good chance that you have been triggered into fight or flight (sympathetic state) or you generally feel unsafe. As a result, your inner critic, planner, perfectionist, self-saboteur, and performer parts might show up to protect you.

Examples of some of the parts that may show up when you are in a freeze response (dorsal vagal state) are procrastination, people pleasing, retreating/playing small, dissociation, hypervigilance, shutdown/sleep, distraction, or addiction.

Your protector parts that show up in each nervous system state will be unique to you, so getting familiar with what they are and in which nervous system state they appear is important. It serves as more information to help you get to know yourself even better.

As previously mentioned, sometimes we overidentify with our parts, and we think we *are* our parts. We are not our parts. The parts are only some of our many fears, emotions, coping mechanisms, defense strategies, avoidance tactics, burdens, etc. The Self is who we truly are.

For example, you may have a people pleaser part which we discussed earlier in chapter eight. If you have identified as a people pleaser, which I know I surely have in the past, then with this new awareness that it is a protector part, I invite you to begin separating your identity from this people pleaser. Recognize it as merely a part of you that has stepped in to keep your Self safe.

If and when you next find your people pleaser part trying to step in and drive your actions, decisions, and behaviors, I want you to notice, observe, acknowledge, and thank your people pleaser for doing such an amazing job of protecting you. You might then use a somatic tool or grounding technique, if necessary, to help you downregulate into a ventral vagal state, allowing your true Self to step forward.

Don't forget to approach this part with compassion, curiosity, courage, and calm. Connecting with the part in this way will help you better understand what it needs and what it is afraid will happen. By doing so, you'll strengthen your connection with your Self and gain greater clarity, confidence, or even creative insights to navigate the path forward. With this deeper understanding, you can ensure that your decisions, actions, and responses align with your highest good, honoring your value, worth, time, and energy without compromise.

Now it is important to note that there are many different protector parts that can show up at any given time and that sometimes more than one may present when triggered.

For example, an anger part, perfectionist part, and an inner critic part may all show up simultaneously when a mistake is made or a perceived failure occurs. The anger part might be internalized, surfacing through the inner critic as harsh, paralyzing self-judgment, berating you for the error and fueling feelings of inadequacy. The perfectionist part, driven by the need to regain control and prevent future mistakes, may overcorrect by working even harder or obsessing over every detail in an attempt to avoid "failing" again. These parts, though seemingly in conflict, are all trying in their own ways to protect you from the pain of shame, rejection, or a perceived loss of worth.

You may be wondering, *Why would making a mistake or failing cause someone to feel unsafe?* As with any trigger, the answer traces back to childhood trauma or adverse childhood experiences. For instance, a person who grew up with overly critical parents who demanded nothing less than perfect grades or insisted on perfect, polite, ladylike behavior in public, may develop a core wound of *I'm not enough, worthy, or important unless I am perfec*t.

When this wound is triggered, protector parts may swoop in to shield against any potential threat. The perfectionist part, for example, may over-effort to prove their value or worth, striving for success or achievement to restore a sense of safety. That safety, however, may only feel attainable when these parts are in overdrive, working relentlessly to avoid failure.

This is why it is so important not only to regulate the nervous system using somatic tools, but also to work directly with these parts. By understanding and harmonizing them, you create a foundation of inner safety that allows for healing and self-compassion.

In a more positive expression, the anger part might serve as a valuable signal to the Self that something is out of alignment and needs attention. The inner critic could offer constructive criticism to encourage the Self to make a good impression or provide the discipline needed to stay focused on the task. Similarly, the perfectionist part could contribute by putting in extra effort, while staying within healthy boundaries, and finding satisfaction in "good enough" rather than striving for or demanding unattainable perfection.

Living life this way, constantly relying on all these parts, can be utterly exhausting. Yet, for many of us, this is how we've learned to survive: by depending on our parts to keep us safe, instead of knowing how to regulate our nervous system and allow the Self to take charge.

The goal of IFS is not to eliminate our parts, but to create harmony among them in an effective and healthy way. This involves communicating with our parts and guiding them to take a supportive role in the backseat rather than allowing them to maintain control and dictate our actions and decisions.

We want to be in Self Leadership, which means connecting with and leading from the Self. The Self is the sovereign part of you that ideally guides all of your other parts. The goal is to develop the ability to make decisions and take actions that align with what is best for your Self, rather than being driven by the fears or wounds of your parts.

When we are in the Self, we embody qualities described in IFS theory as the eight Cs: calmness, clarity, confidence, compassion, curiosity, creativity, courage, and connection. These qualities also align with the experiences we have in a ventral vagal state. Operating from this state of Self Leadership allows us to face life's challenges with resilience, consider different perspectives, resolve conflict, and communicate with intention and effectiveness. It also deepens our capacity to connect vulnerably and authentically with others and ourselves. By cultivating this alignment, we can build healthy, fulfilling relationships, rather than attract toxic or unhealthy dynamics.

This work takes time. It doesn't happen overnight. As I mentioned, the first step is becoming aware of your triggers. When you are triggered into fight or flight (or your sympathetic state, as we discussed in chapter fifteen), the limbic part of your brain is immediately activated, causing your prefrontal cortex to go offline. The limbic system, which is the emotional part of the brain, controls your reactions in these moments. When you're operating from this part of the brain, you become irrational, emotional, reactive, and dysregulated.

Instead of reacting or overreacting to the trigger, try using a grounding technique, a.k.a. a somatic tool, to help you regain your composure and bring your prefrontal cortex back online. Remember, the prefrontal cortex, responsible for logical thinking and problem solving, is rational and reasonable. It also plays a key role in regulating your emotions, which in turn helps to downregulate your nervous system.

The autonomic nervous system (ANS) regulates the body's involuntary functions, including heart rate, breathing, digestion, and perspiration. It responds to stress and other environmental stimuli and is divided into two branches: the parasympathetic, which includes the dorsal vagal and ventral vagal states, and the sympathetic.

As we learned in chapter fifteen, Porges's polyvagal theory explains that the vagus nerve regulates our physiological and emotional responses to stress and social interactions. This means our nervous system communicates with us through our emotions and sensations.

By reflecting on how you felt right before being triggered—and how you felt during the triggering event—you can begin to recognize the physiological and emotional cues your body sends. This awareness helps you notice that you've been triggered even before your cognitive brain identifies what's happening. Over time, you may also become aware of the protector part or parts that show up immediately after a trigger, offering invaluable insight into your internal system.

This exercise can be particularly challenging if you are stuck in a functional freeze state. When triggered into a freeze response, your memory of the event may be blurred because your prefrontal cortex goes completely offline as your body focuses on surviving what it perceives as a life-threatening danger. While your life may not actually be at risk, the subconscious part of your nervous system (the ANS) reacts as though it is. In this state, your hippocampus and prefrontal cortex work to protect you by preventing you from fully processing or remembering the event. Instead, your brain and body prioritize survival over recording the details.

In a freeze state, you are likely to feel dissociated, as if you are completely disconnected from your body and observing reality from a distance, perhaps just above your head. You may feel numb, emotionally detached, or completely shut down, unable to access or process your feelings.

Additionally, you might feel listless, unmotivated, depressed, exhausted, or depleted. This state can leave you feeling uninterested in social connection or drive a desire to self-isolate and withdraw from social settings.

Sometimes, after experiencing chronic abuse, we can become stuck in a freeze state where our nervous system subconsciously perceives life-threatening danger on a regular basis. In this functional freeze state, you may feel like a zombie just going through the motions. It may feel difficult to smile or be present in the moment. While you may be able to manage basic, mindless tasks necessary for survival, you are likely to struggle with clear thinking, focus, creativity, or conflict resolution.

Living in a functional freeze can, over time, feel debilitating. The key to moving out of this state is to actively and consistently use gentle somatic tools such as deep breathing, humming, swaying, rocking, EFT (tapping), or light movement like gentle yoga, stretching, or walking barefoot on grass or sand. Regular use of these tools can help restore your energy and reconnect you with your body.

Once your energy begins to return, you may have to progress to more active somatic movements to release the activation of energy that comes with transitioning from dorsal vagal freeze to sympathetic activation. Practices like dance, vinyasa yoga, jumping jacks, breath of fire, running, brisk walking, connecting with friends, or journaling can help constructively expend this energy. The goal is to continue until you naturally return to a ventral vagal state, where you feel calm, present, focused, motivated, and grounded.

As you work with your triggers, protector parts, and nervous system, you will begin to feel more and more like your Self. By increasing the flexibility in your nervous system and deepening your self-awareness, you build resilience. With resilience, you'll be better equipped to handle life's challenges with strength and confidence.

Chapter Eighteen

HOW TO STOP ATTRACTING NARCISSISTS

Now that you have learned how to identify what a narcissist is, how they are created, and why you may have ended up in a relationship with one, let's focus now on how to *stop* attracting them into your life.

You may have already guessed it (or not), but the first way to start repelling these toxic people from your life is by setting clear and firm boundaries. This may be something you have struggled with, as we have mentioned. It could be because you never learned that setting boundaries is important, or it may not have been something that was modeled for you as a child. Likely your parents didn't have good boundaries, and that dynamic is familiar. The narcissist is also not good at setting boundaries, so again, that dynamic may have been familiar.

So how do you begin to set clear and healthy boundaries?

We will dive more deeply into how to set boundaries in chapter nineteen, but the answer is, you start small. You stop saying yes when you really want to say no. You begin to value yourself, your time, your energy, your needs, your wants, and your desires, and you set appropriate boundaries that reflect your value and worth.

You build the courage to communicate those boundaries clearly and effectively.

You learn to fully love and accept yourself because setting boundaries is an act of self-love.

You understand what healthy love is by cultivating it within yourself *for yourself* and then you stop accepting unhealthy love in the form of breadcrumbs. The pattern of affection and rejection or love and abuse may have been familiar to you from childhood and, as a result, may have created a pain/pleasure addiction or an addiction to chaos. This addiction to the chemicals released during the highs and lows creates a trauma bond, which we discussed previously in chapter nine.

Breaking a trauma bond *can* be done with conscious awareness and intentional effort. It begins with acknowledging the bond and understanding its roots in your past experiences. Trauma bonds thrive on the cycle of intermittent reinforcement—moments of love or kindness intertwined with abuse or rejection. This dynamic creates confusion, leaving you clinging to the hope of change or validation.

To break free, it's essential to create both physical and emotional distance from the source of the bond—the narcissist. This might involve cutting off communication, setting firm boundaries, or seeking support from trusted friends, family, or professionals. Building awareness of your triggers and using grounding techniques, such as breathing techniques or somatic tools, can help you regulate your nervous system and navigate the intense emotions that arise during the process, as discussed in chapter fifteen.

Equally important is reconnecting with yourself. By identifying and healing the core wounds that made you vulnerable to the bond, you can begin to cultivate self-love and self-trust. This inner work empowers you to reframe the narrative, recognize the difference between love and dependency, and prioritize relationships that honor your worth.

Breaking a trauma bond is challenging but deeply transformative. The good news is that this book has already been guiding you through how to break free, so you are already well on your way!

As you release the patterns that no longer serve you, you open space for healthier, more fulfilling connections—beginning with the one you have with yourself.

These steps may feel daunting, but I promise you it *is* possible to break free. I have experienced this transformation not only firsthand, but also in my work with clients. Healing and freedom are within your reach.

The key integral piece to all of this, which we spoke about in chapter fifteen, is... working with your nervous system. Your behavioral patterns were created in childhood as a way to stay safe, as a way to self-preserve. When you begin to learn how to work with your nervous system, you learn how to create safety *within* you, and then you can begin to shift the patterns and feel safe connecting to your true Self.

You'll be less likely to back down on a boundary when you feel like it's safe to maintain it. You'll be more likely to speak your truth, stand up for what you know is right, and stop settling for less than what you deserve when you feel calm, confident, courageous, and clear on who you are, and what you need, want, desire, and value.

When you learn how to regulate your emotions after years of being stuck in a trauma response (a freeze state or constantly walking on eggshells), you'll strengthen your ability to return to your prefrontal cortex, your rational mind, more quickly. This enables you to stay true to YOU, feel safe saying no, and confidently set boundaries in your relationships. With this self-awareness and the use of healthy coping mechanisms, you'll replace maladaptive patterns, like self-sacrificing, with more empowered and supportive choices.

When you are able to set and maintain clear boundaries, you will repel narcissists in your life. You will naturally attract healthy people who are open to fostering healthy relationships that are built upon mutual respect and authenticity.

When you cultivate a strong sense of who you are and learn to fully love and accept yourself, you will no longer compromise your authenticity, values, or value.

When you learn to fill the holes in your own soul and stop seeking outside validation, you will be able to make healthy decisions about what type of behavior you will tolerate and what you will not. You will also begin to attract healthier, more aligned people into your life.

If you've found yourself in these types of relationships, it may be because you have an external locus of control. Once you learn to regulate your internal environment by working with your nervous system, you'll be able to let go of trying to control your external circumstances. This allows you to adeptly handle life's challenges and relationship dynamics with greater ease, without self-abandoning or self-sacrificing.

You'll also be able to set boundaries without fearing an emotional fallout with others.

As you do this work, you'll depersonalize other people's emotions and behaviors, recognizing that their feelings are not your responsibility. If someone becomes disappointed or upset because of a boundary you've set, you'll know how to regulate your own emotions by working with your nervous system. This creates a sense of safety within you so you can continue to reaffirm and reassert your boundaries.

Through this process, you'll increase your ability to trust yourself, reinforce to your doubting mind that you are capable of keeping yourself safe, and consistently affirm your value and worth.

Here is a breakdown of the steps to take in order to begin repelling narcissistic personalities:

1. Cultivate self-awareness: Begin to look deep within yourself to understand your patterns, triggers, and childhood wounds to help you understand why you may seek external validation or feel the need to secure someone else's love in place of cultivating your own self-love.
2. Rebuild your self-esteem: Your self-esteem has likely taken a hit if you've been in a relationship with a narcissist. Look to cultivate your self-worth and value yourself outside of external approval and achievement and independently of anyone else's validation. You are inherently worthy just for being who you are and for no other reason! You don't need to justify your worth, value, or who you are.
3. Set and maintain boundaries: When you set healthy boundaries in your relationships, you foster mutual respect. Learn how to say no and to communicate your needs, wants, desires, and feelings with confidence. It also helps you to feel safe, connecting vulnerably with others so you can create emotional intimacy in your relationships,

which is something a narcissist is not comfortable with. (We will go into more detail in the next chapter.)
4. Foster healthy relationships: Reevaluate your personal relationships. Draw closer to those who respect your boundaries, support your growth, and accept you fully as you are. Place boundaries or move people to your outer circle who do not treat you with mutual respect, reciprocate your level of care and attention, or understand you.
5. Heal your inner child: As we've mentioned, many of your behaviors and coping mechanisms were adapted in childhood. Learn how to reparent your inner child and give them the love, reassurance, protection, validation, and attention they didn't get in childhood so you can heal those childhood wounds.
6. Cultivate unshakable self-love: Cultivate a deep sense of self-love by offering yourself empathy, understanding, and compassion. Treat yourself with kindness and be patient as you heal and recover from narcissistic trauma. Learn to fully self-accept, and in accepting yourself, understand you are not meant to be perfect. No part of you is bad, broken, or damaged. Love yourself for all of your strengths, weaknesses, parts, talents, and flaws. You are perfectly imperfect and lovable just for being you.
7. Educate yourself: Learning and understanding more about narcissism and codependency can help you recognize these unhealthy traits, behaviors, and tactics in the future, so you can avoid unhealthy people. Also, understanding your internal red flags is just as important. Listen to your body and your intuition. They hold more wisdom than your conscious mind could ever know, but it's important to integrate the knowledge *and* the wisdom.

When you learn to cultivate healthy self-love within, you are able to stop attracting unhealthy love externally.

Love yourself enough to know you are worthy of so much more than breadcrumbs.

Chapter Nineteen

BOUNDARIES, BOUNDARIES, BOUNDARIES

This book would be remiss if it didn't include a chapter solely dedicated to boundaries. Boundaries are underrated and rarely recognized for how empowering they can be in your relationships, with both others and yourself.

In part two, if Michelle had set boundaries early on in her interactions with Mike by refusing to answer Mike's calls when they came in at odd hours or communicating that she would only answer his calls during reasonable working hours, she could have possibly avoided the outcome. If she had clearly and firmly stated her boundaries to keep the relationship purely professional, refusing to discuss personal matters, then Mike likely would have backed off. Realizing she could not be easily manipulated or influenced to compromise her own boundaries, he might have saved himself from rejection, embarrassment, and the potential risk of a sexual harassment lawsuit.

Boundaries are the way in which we communicate our limits, needs, preferences, and vulnerabilities. When communicated effectively, they allow us to connect with others on a deeper level because they establish safety in the relationship and provide an opportunity for vulnerability and empathy. You'll understand why shortly. First, we need to lay the groundwork.

Why Are Boundaries Important?

Boundaries help us protect our physical and emotional space so we can be ourselves without fear of exploitation, manipulation, or harm. They may also serve as internal guidelines for how we interact with the world.

When we have well-defined boundaries in our relationships, they become more balanced and mutually respectful. Clear boundaries help reduce anxiety and stress because they eliminate unnecessary confusion and minimize conflict with our partner, loved ones, friends, or colleagues. For example, if you are clear on your partner's boundaries and they are clear on yours, then you'll each understand one another at a deeper level. You'll also feel seen, heard, and respected by your partner as they recognize and uphold your boundaries.

When we set boundaries, we also demonstrate to ourselves and others that our needs and feelings are important. Boundaries are how we advocate for ourselves, communicate what we need, and clearly express what we will or will not tolerate. They empower us to make choices that align with our values and reinforce our sense of self-worth. Boundaries are also an essential part of taking good care of ourselves, as they protect our time, energy, and resources.

Types of Boundaries

There are three different types of boundaries: rigid (hard), porous (soft), and healthy (balanced).

Rigid

Rigid or hard boundaries are more like walls and may refer to limits established around nonnegotiable aspects of your life. While boundaries are important, overly rigid ones can make you appear closed off or detached, working against the goal of fostering emotional intimacy in healthy relationships. People with rigid boundaries often struggle to form close connections with others because their hard boundaries promote emotional distance. Whether intentional or not, rigid boundaries can hinder vulnerability and limit deeper connections. Although rigid boundaries may provide a sense of safety or control, they can also unintentionally limit growth, trust, and connection with others.

With narcissistic or toxic people, rigid boundaries may be entirely necessary and, in fact, mandatory. Narcissists will walk all over your boundaries if you let them, and they'll continue to do so if you've given them even the slightest hint that your boundaries are wishy-washy. Therefore, upholding and setting firm and hard boundaries with the narcissist or other toxic people in your life is important.

An example of a rigid boundary that should remain non-negotiable with a narcissist is refraining from sharing personal or vulnerable information, as it is likely to be used against you. However, in a healthy relationship, withholding such information could hinder the development of emotional intimacy and a close bond with your partner.

Remember, narcissists will likely be the first to push back on your boundaries. In their minds, boundaries do not apply to them because they see themselves as above such limitations. They believe they are entitled to special treatment, so of course your boundaries are irrelevant to them. They will do all they can to bulldoze you into backing down on your own boundaries. However, it's crucial you remain firm. If, after you consistently reasserted your boundaries, they continue to disrespect them, then you may need to issue a consequence. Alternatively, you can protect yourself through internal boundaries by maintaining both physical and emotional distance.

Porous

Porous or soft boundaries are the opposite of rigid or hard boundaries. Porous boundaries may be weak, unclear, or too broad. Someone with porous boundaries may overshare personal information or have a difficult time saying no. They may be easily influenced or persuaded to compromise their boundaries. If you are codependent, then it is likely that your boundaries have been soft, and it may also explain why you attracted the narcissist into your life to begin with. Someone with weak boundaries is more susceptible to manipulation and may allow others to meddle in their problems. Likewise, they, too, may be prone to getting overly involved in someone else's drama. Porous boundaries can result in tolerating disrespect or taking responsibility for someone else's feelings or happiness.

Healthy

Healthy boundaries are more balanced. They are not rigid, nor are they soft. Someone with healthy boundaries will take accountability for their own feelings and actions, while holding others accountable for their behavior. They value their own opinions and respect alternative views, understanding that differences are not a threat. Someone with healthy boundaries will not compromise their value or values for others, nor will they overshare or needlessly withhold personal information. They are open to connection and sharing vulnerably because they are able to set healthy boundaries that create safety, understanding, and respect in their relationships. A person with balanced, healthy boundaries will feel comfortable saying no and accepting another person's no. They recognize that when others say no, it allows the opportunity for someone else, who really wants to be there or who may be more capable, to step in to help. They do not feel guilty setting boundaries; instead, they feel empowered, confident, and secure.

Healthy boundaries are flexible, adapting as trust grows, new information arises, or values or priorities shift in a relationship. The purpose is to create enough safety for you to feel confident and secure in being yourself while also remaining open, vulnerable, and flexible enough to foster genuine intimacy and connection.

Internal Versus External Boundaries

Distinguishing between internal and external boundaries is important. External boundaries are the boundaries you communicate in your relationships that express your needs and preferences. You establish these boundaries by clearly and explicitly defining what you will and will not tolerate to others, for example. Internal boundaries are the internal limits you set for yourself that help you maintain and uphold your well-being, a strong sense of self, and your integrity.

As important as it is to set external boundaries to ensure you are treated with respect and kindness, internal boundaries help ensure you treat *yourself* with the same level of respect, kindness, and compassion. They are crucial for your own sense of inner peace and empowerment.

Internal boundaries help prevent you from self-betraying, self-sabotaging, and breaking your self-trust. Without strong internal boundaries, you may struggle to establish and maintain external boundaries.

An example of an internal boundary would be not feeling responsible for other people's feelings or creating a healthy sleep routine to protect your well-being.

An example of an external boundary would be turning down the opportunity to volunteer for an event you don't have time for or telling someone that you felt unsafe when they raised their voice, followed by requesting that they speak more calmly instead.

In order to set boundaries, it is important to identify what your needs and values are so you can properly articulate and communicate them. In other words, you need to be able to clearly state what it is you need to feel safe, seen, loved, or valued in the relationship.

Understanding your needs, preferences, and values also helps you identify with clarity WHY the boundary needs to be set. Understanding the reason behind a boundary makes it easier to reassert and reaffirm it when someone pushes back or violates it or when you need to set an internal boundary.

Once you have been able to identify your needs, values, and preferences, it's time to start setting boundaries to protect and honor them. Let's dive in.

How to Set Boundaries

1. **Slow Down**
   Learning how to set boundaries takes time and practice. If you notice yourself getting triggered because someone crossed your boundaries, take a moment to assess if either
   a) something got lost in translation and you need to communicate or define your boundary more clearly, or
   b) you need to reaffirm and reassert the boundary.
   When you first start setting boundaries, it can feel overwhelming when someone pushes back or violates a

boundary. Remember, those closest to you may not be used to you setting boundaries, so they, too, will need time to adjust. Stay kind but firm and remind them of the boundary. On the other hand, if you haven't yet identified your non-negotiables, values, or needs, then give yourself some time and space to figure out what they are, so you can identify what boundaries need to be set.

2. **Build Inner Safety**

    This goes back to what we discussed in chapter fifteen. Using somatic tools to help you create safety within yourself by downregulating your nervous system is very important. This way, if someone pushes back on your boundary, causing a guilty part to show up, then you can re-ground and soothe the guilty part so it takes a backseat rather than allowing it to cause you to back down and trip over your own boundaries. Once you've soothed your nervous system with healthy coping strategies like somatic tools, you'll feel safer and more confident to reassert the boundary. Even during conflict, it's important you are able to move out of fight or flight so you can honor and protect your boundaries. You've set them for a reason. **Knowing how to create inner safety helps you cultivate the courage and confidence to ask for what you need and set boundaries regardless of how someone else feels.**

3. **Start Small**

    Just saying no to something you don't want to do (when in the past you may have said yes just to make someone else happy) is a good place to start. It may feel really uncomfortable, and you may feel overwhelmed with guilt, but I promise you it is better to feel guilty than resentful. You can get over guilt much more quickly than resentment, which will simmer below the surface and fester until it poisons you and your relationship. Becoming aware of all the ways in which you overcommit your time and energy and then learning to say no will help you build the confidence to begin setting more boundaries.

4. **Be Clear and Assertive**

Be sure to clearly state your boundaries in a way that honors your intention without leaving any room for negotiation. If your boundaries are unclear, there is a good chance people will try to convince or persuade you to back down. Be firm, be clear, be assertive. You've set the boundary for a reason! If you happen to back down on your boundary, remember to have some self-compassion, as you are still learning. It's never too late to reaffirm your boundary, even if you have backed down. There will be multiple opportunities to set, maintain, and hold your boundaries, which brings us to number five below.

5. **Practice, Practice, Practice**
   As with anything else I've taught in this book, practice makes nearly perfect! The more you continue to set boundaries, the easier it will become. You'll be able to let go of the guilt and feel more confident as time goes by. Remember to forgive yourself when you revert to old patterns; you are learning a new way of being. Then offer yourself some grace and compassion, knowing that there will always be another opportunity to try again.

6. **Keep It Simple**
   You never need to overexplain yourself when setting a boundary. For example, if you say no when someone asks you to do something, do not feel obligated to overexplain or go into a lot of detail about why you are saying no. You have the right to say no without providing an explanation or story. The same goes for any boundary you are setting. You don't need to explain or justify your boundary. If for some reason you feel you need to explain yourself, be sure to keep it concise and do not allow any room for negotiation.

7. **Reflecting Inwards**
   Be sure to tune in to how you are feeling after you set a boundary. Remember, not everyone will accept or respect your boundaries the first time around, especially those who are not used to you setting them. If discomfort arises, allow yourself to feel it fully and then let it go. Stay

curious about the sensations and emotions that surface, and engage compassionately with any protector parts that emerge to help keep yourself safe. These parts may provide valuable insights, such as ways to clarify your boundary or the reasons it's important to reaffirm it if it's challenged.

8. **Seeking Support and Accountability**
Having a safe outlet for your emotions if you are struggling to set boundaries or if you feel uncomfortable or fearful setting them is important. Journaling how you feel or seeking the support of a coach or therapist who can guide you through the process is very helpful. You may also consider keeping a boundary journal to help you recognize the patterns of emotional responses within your relationships and evaluate the strength of your boundaries. It may also help you assess how effective or ineffective your boundaries are, in case you need to craft them more clearly. Getting the right kind of support is important so you avoid falling back into old patterns of behavior and to ensure accountability for enforcing your boundaries.

Further Tips

Use "I" statements: Avoid stating a boundary by commenting on what someone else said or did that upset you. Instead, use an "I" statement to express yourself without assigning blame, which helps prevent the other person from becoming defensive. Using an "I" statement shifts the conversation from becoming confrontational to constructive and productive.

Setting boundaries is an opportunity to vulnerably connect with someone else on a deeper level by sharing how you feel and asking for what you need.

Remember, no one else can *make* you feel anything, just as you can't *make* anyone else feel a certain way. You are responsible for your emotions just as other people are responsible for theirs. It is the perceptions and meanings we have given our past experiences that have informed our thoughts and feelings. Sometimes those perceptions or meanings are distorted from the truth. For example, if you notice that you feel triggered every time someone speaks to you in a loud, angry voice, it may be because as a child, whenever you got in trouble, you were yelled at and spanked for bad behavior. This made you feel unsafe and perhaps unloved, wondering why the people who loved you most, hurt you the most. Therefore, in a relationship, you might need to set a boundary. For example, you may say, "I feel overwhelmed and frightened when you speak to me in an angry tone, and I have a hard time hearing what you are saying because I find myself shutting down. What you have to say is important to me, so when you are ready, I need you to please speak more calmly so I can understand you."

Find the right words and timing: How you communicate your boundary, including your tone of voice, is important. Be sure to be calm (refer back to number two of how to set boundaries above!), clear, and not overreactive when communicating your boundary to increase the chances of it being heard and respected, rather than creating confrontation and confusion. Communicating a boundary in the heat of the moment may not be the best time. It may be best to state your boundary once everyone has cooled off. Sometimes clearly stating that you need some space to calm down for a couple hours is the boundary you need to communicate in order to avoid further confusion, hurt, or misunderstanding.

Remember, boundaries are a communication tool that help you build healthy, interdependent relationships. Being able to set healthy and effective internal and external boundaries is an important tool in your communication toolkit, and those boundaries help you connect more meaningfully with others, so practice, practice, practice.

Boundaries can also help you exit out of the Karpman Drama Triangle that we discussed in chapter eight. If you stop taking responsibility for other people's emotions or meeting their needs ahead of your own, you'll no longer step into the role of the fixer/rescuer or the victim. If you start taking accountability for your own emotions, you'll no longer be the victim or the persecutor. All in all, if you set healthy boundaries, you'll no longer get dragged into the drama of codependency, allowing you to break the patterns and disrupt the cycle of unhealthy relationships that have been so familiar to you.

Conclusion

Right now, I understand you may be feeling a bit overwhelmed, but I promise that as you take one step forward, things will begin to get a little bit easier. You are likely tired of hearing me say this by now but remember to work with your nervous system. If you move too quickly or try to do all the healing at once, you will trigger your nervous system into a shutdown. All you have to do is focus on the very next step—not ten steps down the line—just the very next one. As the old adage goes, "How do you eat an elephant? One bite at a time." So, what small bite or micro-step can you take today?

That step might be taking time for yourself right now. Spend as much time as you need in the cocoon phase. It's okay to spend time alone, away from family and friends, to process your emotions and what you've been through, but please also seek out the professsional support, a coach like me or a therapist well versed in narcissistic abuse, so you're not alone and don't get stuck reliving the past. Talk therapy can be wonderfully validating and helpful for processing trauma. Working with a coach who can provide you with practical tools and strategies to release the trauma from your body and help you move forward is equally important.

Take the time to rest, recharge, process, grieve, release, and rejoice! Don't feel guilty for one minute for taking this time. Think about everything you have been through and how deeply you've been wounded. If those wounds were physical, it might take years for them to heal and for you to fully recover. Treat yourself with kid gloves as your heart is likely very tender. If it feels like your heart is made of steel instead, well then it still needs to be tended to with loving care. Creating the safety within yourself to bring down the iron walls is just as important as it is to create safety around a tender, bleeding heart.

Be sure to nourish your body, mind, and spirit with healthy food, mindfulness practices (being still), daily movement, and spiritual practices that connect you to something bigger than yourself. Take good care of yourself, learn to love yourself before you bring another "love" into your life. Now begins the greatest love affair of your life… the one with yourself! (And no, not in a narcissistic way but in a healthy and much needed way!)

This last part bears repeating because I find so many women who end up getting involved quickly in another relationship after a toxic one ends as a way to distract themselves from the pain. Please, please, please take all the time you need to heal and enjoy the process of falling in love with your Self! Be generous with the amount of time you give yourself to recover. Otherwise, you increase your chances of ending up in another narcissistic relationship. Go back and reread Chapter Eighteen: How to Stop Attracting Narcissists, if you need reminding.

Also, it's essential to grieve the loss of the relationship, even if it was toxic. While, yes, it may feel as though a weight has been lifted off your shoulders and you may even feel happy and free, you have still likely experienced many living losses.

The loss of the relationship you once had before it turned toxic, the loss of the relationship you didn't get to have, and perhaps the loss of companionship or friendship (narcissists aren't always terrible people all of the time) are each significant; allow yourself the time you need to grieve. You may also be grieving other aspects, i.e., the loss of being with your children all of the time, the loss of a home, the loss of the good times, the loss of your in-laws (if you were close), the loss of mutual friends, the loss of spending certain holidays or weekends/weekdays with your kids due to a co-parenting schedule, the loss of a lifestyle, the loss of being part of a couple, the loss of doing couple things (for now!), and the loss of the years spent in an unhealthy relationship, etc.

All of these living losses are important to acknowledge, feel, express, and process. You would do yourself a huge disservice if you tried to numb or distract yourself away from feeling any of it. This is why the cocoon phase is so vital to recovery.

All that being said, we don't want you to get stuck in just grieving either. We also want you to release the anger and resentment and learn how to forgive, when or if you are ready. Forgiveness is not for the other person; it is for you so you can let go and move on. Forgiving someone doesn't mean you forget what happened nor is it saying that what they did to you was okay. It also does not mean you'll look the other way the next time it happens. It means you are letting go of the energy you're using to hold the grudge, which can feel draining. Think about all the other things you could be doing with the energy you are burning through trying to hold on to the resentment. Forgiveness allows us to move from victimhood, where we blame and curse the person who hurt us, to empowerment, where we release resentment, cultivate understanding, take accountability for our own patterns of behavior, and move forward with courage. It allows us to create the next experience we want to have with more love in our hearts, more clarity and determination, and more zest for life because we are no longer allowing the resentment and blame to drain us of our innate essence.

Remaining a victim allows someone else to be in control of our narrative—of our emotions—and attract more of the same (more victims into our life). This is why so many women end up in relationships with another narcissist who also plays the victim (hello, malignant and covert vulnerable narcissists!).

One of my favorite ways to work on forgiveness is through the Hawaiian forgiveness practice of Ho'oponopono.[11]

In this practice, write down what happened, express remorse, and then offer forgiveness to the other person, followed by an expression of gratitude and love. The Ho'oponopono prayer is:

I'm sorry.

---

11 Wailana Kalama, "Hawaii's Trendy Word That's Misunderstood," BBC, September 17, 2018, https://www.bbc.com/travel/article/20180916-hawaiis-trendy-word-thats-misunderstood. This is adapted from the traditional hoʻoponopono which is a process that takes a day or, in some cases, years. It's about a sense of community and communal feeling of responsibility towards an issue. In ho'oponopono, one person's issue becomes the entire group's, and together, with consultation of the group's elders, they find a resolution that is accepted by the whole community. It has been brought into modern spiritual practice as a short, four-line prayer which can be used by any individual as a personal healing prayer of forgiveness for self and others.

Please forgive me.
Thank you.
I love you.

This forgiveness practice is also effective for self-forgiveness, which we also need to do to bring us more peace. Sometimes we don't realize how much self-blame we are carrying as well, which can hold us back.

I understand that forgiveness may feel like something you'll get to at some distant point in the future, but if you can start with self-forgiveness and forgiving small things throughout your day, then you'll eventually find it much easier to forgive those who have hurt you the most. Recognize that we are all human, each doing our best—even when our actions may inadvertently hurt others—and that we are all deserving of forgiveness. Forgiveness goes hand in hand with acceptance. Accepting that the narcissist is who they are and that they are not going to change, even if they appear different on the outside, will also bring you peace. If you continue to maintain even the smallest shred of hope they will change, then sadly you will be disappointed time and time again. When people show you who they are, believe them. Don't try to change the narrative or believe in some fairy-tale ending (thanks, Disney!). Accept them for who they are and if they aren't treating you the way you deserve, move on.

There will be days, much like in the grief cycle, where you feel happy, free, or content, and other days where you feel ovewhelmed, angry, bitter, or resentful. You may also experience days where you feel rejuvenated, alive, or grateful and other days where you feel sad, weepy, or numb and shut down. It can feel like an emotional roller coaster. Having a network of supportive relationships is really important during the cocoon phase but also in the recovery process and life in general. If you are waking up to realize you are surrounded by narcissists, then finding a community you can leverage for support in the meantime will be very helpful. Come join us in Savvy & StrongHER, my online narcissistic trauma recovery group! When you join a community of women who understand what you've been through, you'll feel less alone. Sadly, there are many of us who have been there. It can be very comforting and validating to gather with other women who get it and who are waiting to welcome you with open arms.

Remember, the roller-coaster ride of emotions is all part of the healing experience. You may find that for a period of time you are really angry at your parents for making these relational dynamics familiar. This is also natural; however, always come back to forgiveness. They were acting from *their* wounds and may still be acting from their wounds (self-development has only become more popular in the last ten to fifteen years!). Your parents were behaving at the level of awareness they had in the moment. They likely parented you the way they were raised by their parents. This is why generational trauma exists—because we are each impacted by the wounds of the generation before us, who are impacted by the wounds of the generation before them, etc. We also carry the imprint of trauma in our DNA as described by epigenetics. So, please give them all a pass and know they were doing the best they could, knowing what they knew at the time. They loved you in the best way they knew how, and it's not your job to point out all the mistakes they made or how they can heal from their own trauma. That onus is on them when, and *if*, they are ready. It's all about right timing, and their journey may be different than yours. For now, love and accept them for who they are and forgive them for not being perfect.

The more you can use the somatic tools taught in this book and become aware of which protector parts are showing up when you feel overwhelmed, stressed, or triggered, or where you are in your nervous system, the more you'll be able to regain control over your life rather than letting your emotions, coping strategies, avoidance tactics, and defense mechanisms take over. In time, your confidence and courage will grow, and your ability to set boundaries clearly and effectively will strengthen, as will your ability to make clear decisions about how to move forward as your strong, capable, loving, vulnerable Self.

You will meet people along the way who may pique your interest, whom you want to get to know better, and that's okay, provided you're able to set clear and healthy boundaries. My suggestion is to give yourself *at least* a year before you start dating again for all the reasons aforementioned. You may need more time than that, so reassess after a year or when you feel confident in your ability to make healthy decisions for yourself and have cultivated a strong sense of self-trust.

Getting clear on what you want, need, desire, and value before you allow yourself to get influenced by someone else's wants, needs, desires, and values is so important. Again, establishing a healthy sense of self, before you begin dating, is important so you don't lose yourself again.

As you continue along this journey, you may experience setbacks and pitfalls, but you'll also experience expansion and growth. Remember, even if you are taking five steps forward and three steps back, you are still moving forward. You are a beautiful work in progress!

Life on the other side of narcissistic abuse is full of potential, possibilities, freedom, and safety. Safety *you* are able to create within yourself first. When you become your own rock-solid foundation, you become unshakable. But you also leave plenty of opportunity to build and create something new upon your new foundation. Have fun exploring new hobbies, meeting new people, experiencing new adventures, and entertaining new opportunities as you rediscover your Self.

The people who come into your life will be "bonuses," because you won't need someone in your life; you'll become curious about them in an insatiable way that leads to greater intimacy, more fun, and more pleasure. In a healthy relationship, you lovingly choose your partner every day, and that is easier to do if you remain open with curiosity, empathy, and vulnerability.

As you move away from chasing unhealthy love from others and toward cultivating an unbreakable love within you for YOU, you will attract healthy partners who value you for your authentic Self and whom you will accept and love for who they are authentically. As a result, you'll never feel unseen, unheard, or unloved again.

From this point forward, I hope you are able to heal another piece of your heart, if not fully, then mostly. Healing is certainly not a linear pathway to a destination; it is a journey that involves many twists and turns. Enjoy the ride! The goal is to eventually live as your true Self, fully embodying your sovereignty, authenticity, and power, with a heart that remains courageously open (with boundaries!) and vulnerable to richness of this incredible human experience called life.

Of course, I am here for you, should you need further support. For free resources, please check out my website and podcast, AwakenHer, which is available on all major podcast platforms.

Or head to https://awakenherpodcast.com.

You may also head to my website to connect with me directly.

Or head to https://www.corissastepp.com.

More importantly, if you would like support as you heal and recover, I would love to welcome you into Savvy & StrongHER, which offers a free community tier filled with resources or a higher tier where we do all the healing work we discussed here in this book, but to a much greater degree.

The best part about Savvy & StrongHER is that it is a close-knit community of women who understand what you've been through and who are ready to support and cheer you on along the way. We'd love to have you join us.

Or head to https://bit.ly/stronghermembership.

I also offer one-on-one support. Feel free to book a free call with me to discuss further.

Or head to https://bit.ly/claritycallwithcorissa.

If you'd like to stay connected on social media, be sure to follow me on Instagram @corissastepp.

I wish you the absolute best, and I hope this book has helped you gain a better understanding about who and what a narcissist is, validated your experience in a narcissistic relationship, and informed you with tools necessary to aid in your recovery process. I also hope it has provided you a glimmer of hope that there is so much more to life than what you have experienced thus far! The best is yet to come!

To your growth and expansion and with lots of love,

Corissa

About the Author

Corissa Stepp is a Holistic Trauma Recovery Coach specializing in Narcissistic Abuse who helps accomplished, empathetic women overcome the effects of toxic relationships and reclaim their power. Despite their intelligence and kindness, these women often find their compassion exploited. Corissa empowers them to uncover their hidden strength, rebuild confidence, and create lives filled with love and purpose.

Using Polyvagal Theory, Internal Family Systems (IFS), Human Design, Hypnotherapy, sound healing, and somatic practices, Corissa supports her clients in releasing patterns of trauma that keep them stuck, helping them move forward with clarity and confidence.

As the author and host of the AwakenHer Podcast, Corissa is a voice of hope and renewal. Her mission is to help women turn pain into purpose, reclaim their self-worth, and step boldly into lives defined by self-love, joy, and limitless potential.

For more great books from Empower Press
Visit Books.GracePointPublishing.com

If you enjoyed reading *The Savvy Girl's Guide to Thriving Beyond Narcissistic Abuse,* and purchased it through an online retailer, please return to the site and write a review to help others find the book.